AF743924

The Global Korean Motor Industry

'*The Global Korean Motor Industry* is a welcome and needed contribution to our understanding of the evolution of the global automobile industry in the past decade.' *Thomas A. Kochan, George M. Bunker Professor of Management, Sloan School of Management, MIT Cambridge, Massachusetts.*

'...this volume by Russell Lansbury and his colleagues provides an excellent basis for discussion and a prompt for future work. Their contribution is much appreciated.' *Harry C. Katz, Dean and the Jack Sheinkman Professor, School of Industrial and Labor Relations, Cornell University, Ithaca, New York.*

The book examines the experiences of the globalising Korean automobile industry, with particular focus on the Hyundai Motor Company (HMC), one of the most prominent of the new Korean multinational corporations. It provides an overview of the changing nature of the global automobile industry, before considering in depth the globalisation processes that the Korean automobile industry has undertaken. It traces the development of HMC as it recovered from the failure of its first venture overseas, in Canada, and tried again in India, exploring the similarities and differences between the practices which HMC implemented in India and Korea. It highlights the importance of production systems and employment relations as part of HMC's growth, and argues that if Korean companies such as HMC are to compete successfully as global automobile producers they will need to increase the proportion of overseas production, establish global supply chains and improve co-ordination between head office and subsidiaries.

Russell D. Lansbury is Professor of Work and Organisational Studies and Associate Dean (Research) in the School of Business at the University of Sydney. His recent publications include *International and Comparative Employment Relations* (with G.J. Bamber and N. Wailes), and *After Lean Production: Evolving Employment Relations in the World Auto Industry* (with T.A Kochan and J.P. MacDuffie).

Chung-Sok Suh is Director of the Korea–Australasia Research Centre (KAREC) and Associate Professor in the School of Organisation and Management at the University of New South Wales. He has published widely on the Korean economy, foreign direct investment and international business strategies.

Seung-Ho Kwon is Senior Research Fellow in the school of Organisation and Management, and Associate Director at the Korea–Australasia Research Centre (KAREC) at the University of New South Wales. He is co-author of *The Chaebol and Labour in Korea: The Development of Management Strategy in Hyundai* (W.M. M.O'Donnell).

Routledge Advances in Korean Studies

1. **The Politics of Economic Reform in South Korea**
   A fragile miracle
   Tat Yan Kong

2. **Market and Society in Korea**
   Interest, institution and the textile industry
   Dennis McNamara

3. **Social and Economic Policies in Korea**
   Ideas, networks and linkages
   Dong-Myeon Shin

4. **North Korea in the World Economy**
   Edited by E. Kwan Choi, Yesook Merrill and E. Han Kim

5. **Legal Reform in Korea**
   Edited by Tom Ginsburg

6. **Women, Television and Everyday Life in Korea**
   Journeys of hope
   Youna Kim

7. **Transformations in Twentieth Century Korea**
   Edited by Chang Yun-Shik and Steven Hugh Lee

8. **The Development of Modern South Korea**
   State formation, capitalist development and national identity
   Kyong Ju Kim

9. **Industrial Relations in Korea**
   Diversity and dynamism of Korean enterprise unions
   from a comparative perspective
   Jooyeon Jeong

10. **The Global Korean Motor Industry**
    The Hyundai Motor Company's global strategy
    Russell D. Lansbury, Chung-Sok Suh and Seung-Ho Kwon

The Global Korean Motor Industry

The Hyundai Motor Company's global strategy

Russell D. Lansbury, Chung-Sok Suh and Seung-Ho Kwon

Routledge
Taylor & Francis Group
LONDON AND NEW YORK

30 JAN 2009

338.8872922095195
LAN

First published 2007
by Routledge
2 Park Square, Milton Park, Abingdon Oxon OX14 4RN

Simultaneously published in the USA and Canada
by Routledge
270 Madison Ave, New York, NY 10016

Routledge is an imprint of the Taylor & Francis Group, an informa business

© 2007 Russell D. Lansbury, Chung-Sok Suh and Seung-Ho Kwon

Typeset in Times New Roman by
Newgen Imaging Systems (P) Ltd Chennai India.
Printed and bound in Great Britain by
Biddles Ltd., King's Lynn, Norfolk

BAS066

All rights reserved. No part of this book may be reprinted or reproduced or utilised in any form or by any electronic, mechanical, or other means, now known or hereafter invented, including photocopying and recording, or in any information storage or retrieval system, without permission in writing from the publishers.

British Library Cataloguing in Publication Data
A catalogue record for this book is available from the British Library

Library of Congress Cataloging in Publication Data
Lansbury, Russell D.
The global Korean motor industry : the Hyundai Motor Company's global strategy / Russell D. Lansbury, Chung-Sok Suh, and Seung-Ho Kwon.
p. cm. – (Routledge advances in Korean studies ; 10)
Includes bibliographical references and index.
1. Automobile industry and trade – Korea (South) – Case studies. 2. International business entrprises – Korea (South) – Management – Case studies. 3. Globalization – Economic aspects – Korea (South) – Case studies. I. Hyondae Chonghap Sangsa (Korea) II. Suh, Chung-Sok, 1957– III. Kwon, Seung-Ho, 1964– IV. Title.

HD9710.K64H965 2007
338.8'8729222095195–dc22 2006023112

ISBN10: 0–415–41366–4
ISBN13: 978–0–415–41366–4

This book is dedicated to the memory of Soo-Eun Kim (1975–2003), the late wife of Seung-Ho Kwon.

Contents

Figures

Tables

Foreword

The Global Korean Motor Industry is a welcome and needed contribution to our understanding of the evolution of the global automobile industry in the past decade. We have seen a falling off of studies like this since the early to mid-1990s. During that time all the debate focused on the effects and reach of the Toyota model, following the publication of the MIT study, *The Machine that Changed the World*. But the last decade's developments have been dominated by Hyundai's growth, as much if not more so than Toyota's. Yet we know very little about the actual workings of Hyundai, and we are especially lacking in our understanding of its strategies and operations outside of Korea, where it is increasingly placing its production facilities. So we badly need a careful and well-documented study of this emerging giant in the industry.

The careful research contained in these chapters helps us understand how and why Hyundai has grown rapidly. The in-depth study of the Indian operations gives us a window on how the company is operating in this developing economy, in particular.

This book will also be of interest to scholars and professionals beyond the auto industry. The authors show how Hyundai is adapting its Korean employment practices in ways both consistent with prevailing practices in autos (thereby showing some converging tendencies) and yet carrying over its management style (authoritarian and control of labour, union avoidance, etc.) and fitting it into the Indian setting, thereby showing the divergent effects of company and local cultures and institutions. Thus, the book contributes to the on-going debate among researchers and international experts on how globalisation is playing out in different settings.

Thomas A. Kochan,
George M. Bunker Professor of Management,
Sloan School of Management, MIT, Cambridge, Massachusetts

Acknowledgements

We are grateful for the support for this project from the *Australian Research Council* and the *Korea Research Foundation*. We are also grateful for the kind assistance given by a number of employees of the Hyundai Motor Company (Korea) and Hyundai Motor India.

Several colleagues provided valuable research assistance to the project, including Professor William Purcell, University of Newcastle, as well as Debra Da Silva, Christopher Wright, Clare Yazbeck and Bronwyn Hudson (all at the University of Sydney). Rawya Mansour (University of Sydney) provided significant assistance with the preparation of the manuscript. Finally, Peter Sowden showed his faith in our work by accepting our book for publication and providing expert advice. Owen Lansbury designed the book cover. Thanks are also due to other colleagues at the University of Sydney and University of New South Wales for their interest and encouragement.

1 Introduction

In recent decades, multinational enterprises (MNE) increasingly dominated global production as they expanded their foreign direct investment (FDI) in order to secure global competition advantages and overcome regional market protection. The automobile industry is a prime example of globalisation in which auto manufacturers have developed networks, alliances and cross-shareholdings across regions and nations. From the end of the Second World War until the mid-1960s, US producers dominated the auto industry with their vast domestic market and expansion into Europe and elsewhere. Yet by the 1970s, Japanese auto firms, led by the Toyota Motor Company, had begun not only to penetrate North America but were also capturing new markets in Europe and Asia. By the end of the 1980s, the Toyota Production System was declared to be the dominant paradigm by the influential book *The Machine that Changed the World* in which Womack *et al.* (1990) coined the term 'lean production'. Toyota demonstrated that it was possible to continuously improve production processes while building relatively cheap models of high quality. During the 1990s, Japanese auto companies shifted their strategy of exporting from Japan to building transplant facilities overseas in order to produce vehicles in other countries. Japanese auto firms gradually outstripped their US rivals in their share of the world market and by the mid-1990s accounted for one third of all vehicle sales in the United States.

The rise of the Japanese auto industry as a dominant global force, and the example of the Toyota Motor Company in particular, revived the concept of the 'world car'. This first emerged in the 1970s when US companies forecast that great economies of scale could be achieved by the production and sale of the same products across different markets around the globe. Subsequently, however, the lean production system, developed by Toyota, was hailed as the 'one best way' to organise the manufacturing of automobiles and other companies were exhorted to either adopt Toyota's techniques or fall by the wayside in the increasingly competitive world market.

The view that lean production would become the new global paradigm for auto manufacturing had implications for employment relations practices. Lean production has been defined as 'an interrelated set of technological, organisational and human resource policies that, when implemented together, constitute a new flexible system of work' (Womack *et al.* 1990). This is contrasted with mass production which is regarded as a more rigid, supply-oriented system less able to react to changes in market conditions, product life cycles and consumer tastes. Lean production also emphasises the effective utilisation of human resources to avoid excessive labour, which can mean fewer workers undertaking a wider range of tasks. This aspect of lean production has been criticised as both 'lean and mean' because there is excessive pressure and stress on the workforce. Concern has been raised by critics of globalisation that multinational enterprises in the auto sector will engage in a 'race to the bottom' by reducing wages and conditions and seeking to erode labour standards. There is also a view that lean production is simply an old fashioned 'speed-up' production device designed as a new idea in order to more subtly control the workforce, strengthen the role of management and weaken the trade unions (Babson 1992).

The more dramatic forecasts about globalisation of the auto industry have not yet been realised. Attempts to create a 'world car' have encountered significant obstacles. The demand for standardised models of automobiles has stabilised and declined. Even some of the Japanese companies which were initially successful in marketing a homogenised product to all their markets have changed to local adaptation of models. It appears that regional rather than global strategies offer considerable opportunities to auto companies and a number have abandoned their previous policies of a worldwide approach to production. The dominance of lean production has also been questioned as local conditions and practices have proved to be resistant to change and demonstrated that there is not necessarily a single set of best practices for assembling motor vehicles. Indeed, while lean production has proved to be a most efficient and effective system in some circumstances, mass production persists and there are also many examples of hybrid combinations of mass and lean production systems.

One of the key features of the changing nature of the global automobile industry is the saturation of traditional markets in North America, Europe and Japan and the expansion of production and growth of sales in emerging markets such as Asia and South America. Annual auto production at a global level has increased from 18 million in the mid-1960s to 44 million in 2004, but the demand for new vehicles in the 'triad' markets of North America, Europe and Japan is growing at only 2 per cent per annum. However, vehicle production in newly emerging industrial economies such as China and India have doubled in the past four years and these two countries are likely to be ranked third and fourth in the world league of auto producers within a decade. Although many of the companies which are establishing new plants in China and India are based in the United States and Europe, the 'big three' – General Motors, Ford and Daimler-Chrysler – are all encountering financial difficulties and only Toyota appears to be secure. Hence, it may be companies from Japan and relatively new entrants such as Hyundai from Korea which are best positioned to capitalise on new opportunities in China and India.

Whether multinational auto companies are adopting particular production systems in their newer plants in India and China, and how these impact on their employment relations systems, has yet to be systematically studied. However, it is apparent that the strategies pursued by the multinationals are not uniform and cannot be assumed to necessarily follow a predictable course. It is important to pay close attention not just to the espoused policies of different companies but also to how these policies are translated into practices.

Ferner and Edwards (1995) reported that the diffusion of common employment practices within multinational corporations varied according to their organisational characteristics and some were more likely to seek homogenisation than others. Frenkel (1994) argued that similarities which he observed in four plants owned by the same multinational pharmaceutical company could be explained by a combination of factors 'internal' and 'external' to the organisation. Among the former, he regarded managerial strategies and the relations between head office and subsidiary managers as vital, but their impact was influenced by national industrial relations institutions and other external factors like product markets. Edwards *et al.* (1999) offered a similar but more sophisticated argument when they highlighted the 'bi-directional' relationship between 'structural factors' – like markets, production systems and management structures – and 'political processes' internal to the organisation – such as the ambitions and strategies of individual managers, and the success or failure of struggles between head office and managers of subsidiary organisations. In their study of several plants of Asea Brown Boveri (ABB) around the world, Bray and Lansbury (2000) found that while there was a general tendency towards harmonisation of employment relations practices, there remained elements of national and local diversity that were unlikely to entirely disappear. MacDuffie's study of the world auto industry, which examined both production systems and employment relations, also noted how influences from the parent company towards uniformity interacted with factors in the national context which strengthened local differences. MacDuffie concluded that 'it may make sense to first examine company-level factors affecting the adoption and diffusion of new approaches to work organisation and then to turn to national level explanation to explain residual variation' (MacDuffie 1995: 106).

It is apparent from these studies that globalisation is not a 'monolithic juggernaut leading inexorably to common judgements across different national regimes' (Bray and Murray 2000). Yet clearly there are common pressures arising from the expansion of FDI, the adoption of new production systems and the growing significance of multinational enterprises. Based on their studies of both the auto and telecommunications industries in six countries, Katz and Darbishire (2000) concluded that there were 'converging divergences' characterised by the spread of four patterns of workplaces processes: low wages, HRM, Japanese-oriented and joint-team-based approaches. However, they also highlighted differences in the distribution of these patterns at the national level as well as in the extent of variation within countries. While there have been criticisms of the converging divergences approach, Katz and Darbishire's work highlight the importance of interaction between both convergent and divergent tendencies in employment relations. In a similar vein, Bamber *et al.* (2004) argue for an *integrated* approach that focuses on the interaction between market and institutional variables which shape employment relations outcomes.

The case study reported in this book traces the emergence of the Hyundai Motor Company (HMC) from a complete knock down (CKD) assembler, under an agreement with the Ford Motor Company in 1968, to one of the world's top 10 manufacturers. In 1976, HMC produced its first originally designed model, the *Pony*, using a low-cost strategy. Less than 10 years later, in 1985, HMC opened its first overseas plant in Canada in order to assemble the mid-sized, front wheel drive *Sonata* model.

Like Korea's other major family-owned conglomerates, known as the *chaebols*, HMC increased its FDI in Asia during the early 1990s as part of its growth strategy. Until the mid-1990s, HMC focused mainly on exporting domestically produced vehicles but realised that it needed to move off-shore if it was to become a major international competitor. HMC adopted the strategy pioneered by the Japanese auto companies, more than a decade earlier, of entering at the lower end of the market and moving upwards. Gaining a secure market share was more important than creating short-term profit, and HMC was willing to commit considerable financed resources to achieve success. HMC sought to introduce some elements of the Japanese management system but it adopted a mass production system rather than the lean production principles pioneered by Toyota. HMC opened its first overseas plant in Canada in 1985 but closed it in 1993 after prolonged operational and industrial relations problems. In 1996, HMC established a 100 per cent-owned subsidiary in Chennai, India, and constructed a plant designed to build 120,000 passenger cars a year.

The objective of this case study is to analyse the experience of Hyundai Motors India (HMI) as an example of a Korean firm seeking to 'produce beyond borders' and become a global company. It traces the development of HMI from 1996 to 2001 in order to examine the inter-relationship between FDI, production systems and employment relations in a Korean company attempting to 'go global'. It explores the similarities and differences between production systems and employment relations applied by Hyundai in India in comparable plants in Korea. It seeks to assess the extent to which the company has adapted its system to local circumstances as part of its global strategies of investment and manufacturing. This will provide insight into the approaches adopted by a major Korean *Chaebol* as it extends its activities on a global scale.

2 The global auto industry

The development of integrated global manufacturing in the automobile industry depends on a variety of factors associated with product markets and production processes. The location decisions of multinational enterprises (MNEs) are also a vital consideration. Debate exists about how far global manufacturing has actually occurred in the automobile industry. The concept of a 'world car' pioneered by the Ford Motor Company was based upon relatively standardised products being built from standardised component parts, common production systems across countries and location decisions that would yield cost advantages in economies of scale and specialised plants.

The question as to the extent to which automobile production has become globalised may be assessed by referring to UNCTAD's transnationality index. This index is calculated as the average of three ratios. These are the share of a company's foreign assets to total assets, the share of overseas sales to total sales and the levels of employment abroad compared to total employment (UNCTAD 1999). It may come as a surprise that according to the transnationality index the automobile industry is less internationalised than various other industries, including food production, chemicals and electronics.

Nevertheless, the automobile industry is typically considered to be at the forefront of globalisation. Evidence supporting this view includes: the intricate network of alliances and cross-shareholdings among automobile companies, within nations and regions but also between regions (Vickery 1996), intensified merger and acquisition activity in the 1990s involving both end-producers and automobile input suppliers (PricewaterhouseCoopers 2000a; World Trade Agenda 2000), the trend towards technologically motivated cooperation agreements, which was caused, inter alia, by end-producers entering into new forms of partnerships for the design of principal components and subsystems (UNCTAD 1999: 25) and the significant role of intra-firm trade, for example, of US-based automobile multinationals (UNCTAD 1999: 443).

The growth in demand for automobiles around the world varies considerably. As shown in Table 2.1, traditional markets for automobile production, such as Europe and North America, have grown by approximately 1.5 per cent in recent years. By contrast, emerging markets such as China have been growing by an annual rate of almost 19 per cent and are still expanding. These emerging

Table 2.1 Production trends by original equipment manufacturers in the automobile industry by regions, 2001–2007

Region	*2001*	*2003*	*2005*	*2007 (forecast)*	*Annualised growth rate (%)*
Europe	19,167,285	18,805,984	20,125,123	20,717,034	1.43
Japan and Korea	12,000,932	12,472,631	12,727,279	13,050,067	1.48
North America	15,528,555	15,895,368	16,366,942	17,093,866	1.51
South America	2,088,541	1,956,746	2,337,253	2,527,842	3.80
Emerging markets	4,788,571	6,908,481	9,214,194	10,879,879	18.97
Total global production	53,573,884	56,039,210	60,770,791	64,268,688	3.12

Source: www.csmauto.com third quarter 2003 forecast.

markets, while attractive in terms of the number of consumers, also present challenges for the manufacturers due to the heterogeneity of demand. The supply side of the automotive industry has seen a number of automotive manufacturers form global alliances in order to gain an increased share of both traditional and new markets, to research and design cross-platform vehicles, to achieve economies of scale and ultimately, to protect shareholders' value. Other issues on the supply side include the globalisation of components and parts manufacturing, and the resultant impact that this has had on local industry and labour markets, the increased access to technology and research and development (R&D), the management of supply chains, the shift from mass production to lean production and the localisation of production facilities.

Changes in the worldwide automotive industry

The past decades have witnessed major changes in the world automobile industry. In the mid-1960s, the 'big three' US auto companies (General Motors, Ford and Chrysler) were 'kings of the road' with a vast domestic market under their domination and almost half the total world production of motor vehicles (Kochan *et al.* 1997). The combined output of all European automobile plants accounted for 40 per cent of the world's automobiles, although these included plants owned by US auto companies. The Japanese auto companies, which would emerge as major players in the 1970s and 1980s, produced less than 10 per cent of vehicles in the total world automobile market by the mid-1960s.

International trade between auto-producing countries in the 1960s was still small scale and involved mainly niche specialty products. Domestically produced vehicles still accounted for 90 per cent of sales. When GM and Ford began to extend into Europe they did not export vehicles from the United States but developed parallel and independent manufacturing operations in Britain and Germany. By the late 1960s, Ford Europe had pioneered a new kind of multinational factory network with final assembly lines in one European country fed with gear boxes, engines and parts that had been assembled by Ford plants in other European countries. When the European companies began to penetrate the US market with smaller cars, the American manufacturers retaliated by developing their own range of smaller cars, known as 'compacts' (see Williams *et al.* 1994).

By the 1970s, manufacturing autarchy had been eroded as trade barriers were lowered and differences in product size and packaging were reduced. The liberalisation of world trade under the General Agreement on Tariffs and Trade (GATT) and the creation of regional free trade zones forced auto companies both to share domestic markets with new foreign entrants and to compete with other firms in virtually all major markets. Market fragmentation began in the United States with small fuel-efficient European imports in the wake of the oil crisis during the early 1970s, despite resistance by US manufacturers. By the end of the 1970s, the 'big three' US auto companies (GM, Ford and Chrysler) had lost substantial market share to Toyota, Honda and Nissan. As the volume of international auto trade increased, the losers were the United States and the United Kingdom. The winners were Japan and Germany, which escaped the limits of their national markets and managed to export more than half their total output. Exports by British carmakers collapsed from 38 per cent in 1979 to 7 per cent in 1990, while Germany consolidated its position as a major exporter of cars by expanding their sales in both the European and North American markets. Overall, while less than 20 per cent of cars produced by the major manufacturing markets entered into international trade in 1960, it had increased to one-third by 1990, most of which was due to Japanese and German auto exports.

The 1980s saw the ascendancy of Japanese carmakers as they gained market shares in North America and established a stronger production presence in Europe, Australia and parts of Asia. Efficiency and high quality, based on the Toyota Production System or 'lean production' as it became popularly known, set the tone of the debate for how automotive manufacturers would compete well into the new millennium. In North America, the 'big three' were facing severe competitive and financial crises (Kochan *et al.* 1997). Likewise, European manufacturers faced a competitive crisis from Japanese manufacturers and a campaign was led by Peugeot to prevent Japanese companies from building plants in Europe or increasing imports to the EU (MacDuffie and Pil 1997).

Although the past three decades have included a number of takeovers and mergers between the international auto producers, the end of the 1990s witnessed the development of strategic alliances based on cross-shareholding rather than acquisitions and mega mergers. Six major alliances, centred on GM, Ford, Daimler–Chrysler, Toyota, Renault and Volkswagen, accounted for 83 per cent of world output in terms of 1998 units. Except for Toyota, each alliance included one or more major allied enterprises. It has been predicted that these alliances will shape the future of the industry, but it should be noted that many alliances are fragile and further changes are inevitable as evidenced by the break-up of the BMW–Rover alliance and difficulties in the merger between Daimler Benz and Chrysler.

Since the late 1990s and following the Asian economic crisis of 1997–1998, other auto manufacturers have begun to catch up to the Japanese producers. During the 1990s, Japanese, Korean and East European auto companies experienced difficulties while American and other European companies embarked upon recovery. In an industry characterised by constant change, the period since the late 1990s has witnessed a new era of global expansion, consolidation and a decline in production among a number of the major producers. This process, however, is uneven and has wide-ranging implications for globalisation within the industry.

Stagnating demand and worldwide overcapacity in the automotive industry

Currently, approximately 12 per cent of the world's 6 billion people enjoy the benefits of automobile ownership and it is expected that industry growth will continue at about 20 per cent per decade, with the potential for global annual sales of 65 to 70 million vehicles by 2010 (Howell and Hsu 2002: 43). Most of this expansion is expected to occur in emerging markets such as China, Brazil, India and Russia. While these markets currently account for only a very small percentage of vehicle sales per year, it is expected that this will increase substantially over the next 10 years. This is due to the main problem facing the automotive industry today, which is stagnating demand in existing markets. This has resulted in increased competitive pressures on auto companies to capture newly emerging markets.

Stagnating demand in mature markets is not simply a cyclical phenomenon, such as economic recessions in Europe and Japan. Rather, it reflects a saturation of demand for automobiles in these markets, with the estimated growth rate in these markets not exceeding 2 per cent between 2001 and 2007 (see Table 2.1). It has been estimated by PricewaterhouseCoopers (2000b) that excess production capacity is approximately 24 million units globally. Given the saturation of such markets and the emergence of excess production capacity (estimated to be more than 2 million units in Europe) with the arrival of new producers, manufacturers have sought out emerging markets in newly industrialising countries (Freyssenet and Lung 2000).

The saturation of traditional markets is affecting vehicle sales. By 2000, a total of 54.7 million units were sold on an annual basis. North American sales increased by 9 per cent to reach a record of 19.7 million units. Asian sales also increased and showed healthy signs of recovery after the Asian economic crisis. There were increased sales in Europe, especially France and Spain, but at a slower rate of growth. This suggests a redistribution of production and demand. Asian countries outside of Japan are steadily increasing vehicle production. In 1990, for example, only a little over 7 per cent of the word's vehicles were produced in this region; by 1994, this had increased to almost 11 per cent. Despite slow sales throughout most of the early 1990s, Asian countries, excluding Japan, purchased more vehicles than they produced and expanded their exports in the second half of the decade. By contrast, production in Japan declined to below the 10 million-unit mark in 2000 for the first time in 20 years, declining by 27 per cent since 1990 (IMF 2000).

A report by the International Metalworkers Federation (IMF) (2000: 8) noted that despite their size, the 'triad' markets (North America, Europe and Japan) are disadvantaged by their maturity and because their sales are primarily for replacement vehicles. On the other hand, the emerging and transitional markets offer better growth opportunities. There has also been expansion of production and sales in the former Communist states of Europe and growth in new markets in the Asia-Pacific Region. However, some commentators argue that these new markets will soon reach over-production (Garibaldo and Battaglini 1998).

The stagnation of demand in mature markets and the problem of worldwide overcapacity in the industry have led manufacturers to develop several strategies on both the demand and supply side. From the demand-side perspective, new emerging markets are expected to account for the majority of growth in demand. Accompanying this strategy is the need for homogenisation of products in order to maintain profit margins through high volume and economies of scale. On the supply side, manufacturers have focused on containing and reducing costs. This cost pressure has forced all manufacturers to reduce structural costs, reduce cycle times for product development, form alliances with other manufacturers and develop products with more innovative styling and content (Howell and Hsu 2002). In addition, auto companies are increasingly looking towards services to increase their profits. Automobile firms have traditionally been involved in service provision (finance, insurance, rentals, used vehicles sales) but are now finding that services, especially the financing of new and used cars, are contributing more to their profitability. Ford's financial division, for example, contributed more than 40 per cent of the group's total operating revenues between 1988 and 1998 (Lung 2001: 101–102).

The attempt to create a 'world car'

The drive for volume growth and search for economies of scale, combined with established market maturity, has required automobile manufacturers to seek emerging markets. However, mature and emerging markets are characterised by different types of demand. In mature markets, demand is typically replacement demand and the recent growth in the North American market has been in the large and luxury cars, sport utility vehicles and truck segments. In emerging markets, demand is typically incremental, as personal transport aspirations are met for the first time. This growth will be dominated by smaller vehicles, generally with low feature content. Consumers in the emerging markets typically have lower incomes compared with consumers in the mature markets of North America, Japan and Europe. The primary driving force behind the purchasing of vehicles is the need for basic transport. However, the production of small, inexpensive vehicles yields only slim profit margins for the manufacturer. Opportunities for greater profitability increase with the volume of production. However, intense competition in the emerging markets may result in profits remaining low.

The demand for mass-produced, standardised models has stabilised and even declined in the traditional markets of volume producers. Recent years have seen the fragmentation of the range of automobile products and the development of secondary product markets. Companies pinning their hopes on servicing the growth in the luxurious, executive and sports car range of segments within developed nations failed to anticipate the growing demand for monospaces and recreational vehicles. Consumer desires for vehicles that reflect their values and lifestyles caused an explosion in demand for recreational, semi-recreational and niche market vehicles. On the other hand, structural adjustment and economic liberalisation in new markets like those in the Asia-Pacific region encouraged large international auto producers to compete with indigenous producers in the small car segment providing 'no frills and value for money'.

Economies of scale in auto manufacturing are achieved by the production and sale of the same products across different markets, rather than the sale of country- or region-specific products. The American global car strategy which sought to create a 'world car' by the 1970s was a response to successful Japanese incursions into various markets (Maxcy 1981). The aim was to produce and sell a vehicle in the major markets that responded to the expectations of consumers, sharing a number of components whilst accepting local adaptations (Freyssenet and Lung 2000). This strategy, which was initiated by Ford, is now being taken up by GM. To a certain extent, Japanese companies are involved in a reverse strategy of pursuing a current strategy of local adaptation of models, whereas they had previously marketed a homogenous product throughout all of their markets (Mair 1994).

The 'world car' concept only has validity if it can be applied to all similar markets or where the vehicle attributes are acceptable to diverse markets but not necessarily occupying the same market position (PricewaterhouseCoopers 2000b). Fiat has exemplified this with its *178* small car programme specially developed for emerging markets. The most successful transference of identical vehicles across global markets occurs where global brand equity is acknowledged, such as BMW, Mercedes-Benz and Porsche (PricewaterhouseCoopers 2000b). However, this is more attributable to successful brand management in niche markets than the existence of homogenous consumer preferences on a global scale.

Analyses of the automobile industry have explored the ideas of homogenisation and heterogenisation on both regional and global levels, and their implication for automobile demand and product markets. The theory of global homogenisation suggests that liberalisation and economic exchange will lead to the homogenisation of automobile markets. This has been given further impetus with the opening up of Japan and ASEAN countries working towards free trade for automobiles. Regionalisation and regional heterogenisation are based upon a policy of specific product range and specialisation within each region (such as the EU, ASEAN etc.) that would promote growth (Boyer *et al.* 1996). While global homogenisation of product markets is the preferred ideal for most large volume auto producers, the reality tends to suggest that this goal is not yet achievable.

An alternative view is that 'worldwide homogenisation in demand is not just around the corner' (Boyer and Freyssenet 2001: 61). The failure of Ford's 'world vehicles', the problems faced in the implementation of worldwide platforms and the reluctance of other manufacturers to adopt worldwide product strategies are all counter-tendencies to the 'world car' concept. Indeed Ford has recently abandoned its worldwide vehicle policy. Instead, it seems that regional rather than global strategies may offer more opportunities for many auto companies. Most vehicle markets, especially in the high-volume model segment, are still primarily regional (Lung 2001).

From mass production to lean production

The growth of international trade in the automobile industry has been facilitated not only by the reduction of tariffs but also by changes in the nature of production systems. Standardised mass production of cars, associated with Henry Ford (and 'Fordism'), reached its most developed form in the large and relatively insulated North American market, which relied on economies of scale for its competitive advantage. Ford first developed the concept of an integrated manufacturing plant at Highland Park in 1911, where an entire car was assembled under one roof and all components were produced at the same location. Ford later extended the principle of integrated, single-site manufacturing to other plants. By the 1980s, however, it was clear that Toyota and other Japanese firms had developed a superior model of organisation which would prove to be the successor to traditional Fordist mass production. This new approach to automobile manufacturing was variously termed flexible specialisation (Piore and Sabel 1984), lean production (Womack *et al.* 1990) and innovation-mediated production (Kenney and Florida 1993).

The 'post Fordist' approach to automobile manufacturing may be broadly described as incorporating the following characteristics: close integration of all parts of the production process, rapid product and process innovation, efficient small-lot production, continuous efforts to enhance quality and productivity at all organisational levels including the shop floor and close integration with suppliers and customers (Deyo 1996).

The Japanese automobile manufacturers pioneered this new approach in response to constraints that they experienced in the implementation of Fordist mass production. They had few opportunities for economies of scale because many companies were competing in a small market and labour costs were fixed as a result of life-time employment agreements (MacDuffie and Pil 1997: 11). However, the Japanese firms turned these 'disadvantages' to their benefit by responding quickly to market shifts and instability, continuously improving productivity and quality through constant changes in work processes and organisation, manufacturing a large number of differential products for diverse export markets and market niches and rapidly developing new products. As a result of these innovations, by the late 1980s Japanese auto companies were producing twice as many models as their US and European counterparts, were replacing models every four years (rather than nine years by the 'big three'), were achieving normal quality standards with new models after two months (compared with twelve months for US companies) and had very low levels of quality defects (Womack *et al.* 1990).

By the late 1970s, Japan had become the world's second largest producer of automobiles and had strongly penetrated the US domestic market. Following the example which US car manufacturing had set many years before, Japanese firms began to establish 'transplant' facilities to produce cars in the United States and the United Kingdom. By the early 1990s, Japanese vehicle manufacturers accounted for 28 per cent of the world market (compared with 21 per cent produced by US companies) and were responsible for one-third of all sales in the United States.

Japanese firms shifted their strategy from exporting from Japan to foreign direct investment (FDI) in other countries during the 1990s. Yet, by the middle of that decade, as other producers also entered the market, their share of world production declined to 21 per cent. Despite this, key elements of the Toyota production system had become widely accepted by auto companies around the world as the key to their survival. This was assisted by the publication of a book

The Machine that Changed the World (Womack *et al.* 1990) based on research conducted in the International Motor Vehicle Programme (IMVP) at MIT, which argued that lean production was the one best way to organise the production of automobiles. Failure to adopt these principles, it was claimed, would result in firms falling by the wayside in an increasingly competitive world market.

While the new paradigm of lean production has been the subject of considerable debate and controversy, particularly in regard to its implications for workers, it has been widely adopted as a set of guiding principles by many automobile manufacturers and has enhanced the process of stabilisation. Critics of lean production have viewed it as an example of neo-Fordism (rather than post-Fordism) which is essentially a 'speed-up' production system dressed up as a new idea: a modern version of Frederick Taylor's methods of controlling the workforce and maximising managerial control (and profits) on the backs of workers. Sceptics doubt that lean production will sweep across the world as predicted. They emphasise the importance of local conditions, institutional factors and changing work practices and reject theories that suggest there is one best way or single set of best practices for performance of any kind, including automobiles. The crisis in the Japanese auto industry in the 1990s suggests that lean production is, at best, only an 'ideal'.

It would appear that firms are not simply choosing between a Fordist (or neo-Fordist) mass production approach and a Toyota-inspired lean production system (which may or may not be post-Fordist). Rather, there is a much broader range of alternatives emerging as a result of interaction between production systems, employment relations systems, competitive strategies and managerial traditions of various firms and the roles played by governments and unions. While there may be a general trend towards the adoption of lean production principles across the auto industry, the actual range of adoption and diffusion is determined by how global competitive processes interact and align with strategies chosen by firms, governments and labour representatives involved. Data from IMVP surveys analysed by MacDuffie and Pil (1997) reveal that although there has been a convergence between firms around matters of principle (such as the desirability of lean production), there has been a diversity of ways in which this convergence has been achieved. The process of moving from mass production to lean production is often incremental or piecemeal in nature. This pattern has given rise to various hybrid arrangements rather than a single new paradigm (see Boyer and Freyssenet 1995). Nevertheless, it is useful to summarise the general principles which distinguish flexible or lean production from traditional mass production (see Table 2.2).

The conclusion from research cited here is that while powerful economic forces related to the globalisation of markets and the influence of FDI have provided a degree of convergence towards flexible or lean production, many factors continue to reinforce constraints on convergence; these have been superseded by more firm-specific factors which reinforce differences. Indeed, MacDuffie and Pil (1997) argue that the auto industry worldwide is composed of four distinct groups of plants and companies. First, Japanese-owned plants in Japan and overseas

Table 2.2 Characteristics of mass production versus flexible or lean production

Characteristics	*Mass production*	*Lean or flexible production*
1 Specialisation of resources and definition of tasks	Extreme specialisation and narrow definition of tasks	More use of general resources, multi-skilling and general purpose machines
2 Standardisation of product design and manufacturing	Highly standardised to permit large batch production	Small lot sizes and buffers to facilitate greater variety
3 Degree of centralisation	Centralised hierarchy to control and co-ordinate tasks	Decentralised authority and lateral communication
4 Separation of conception from execution of tasks	'Thinking' work is separated from 'doing'	Integration of 'thinking' and 'doing' work

Source: Adapted from MacDuffie and Pil (1997).

which adopted lean production principles early and have deepened their use of these practices; second, plants in Europe and some new entrant countries (such as Korea) which are moving away from traditional mass production practices towards more flexible approaches; third, the US-owned plants in North America which have combined (or even returned to) traditional practices and fourth, plants across all regions that manifest some hybrid combination of mass production and lean production practices.

Globalisation of technology and platform sharing

Combining elements of lean production with global competitive influences, as well as the development of strategic alliances amongst the largest producers, suggests the possibility of a new era of automotive production. In order to reduce costs and to remain competitive in the 'new economy', automotive producers have adopted 'techno-globalisation' consisting of global technology networks and technical alliances (Miller 1994: 27). Nowhere is this more evident than in the globalisation of research and development. New techniques have reduced the range of motors, power trains and platforms and there has been a divergence in global and regional outlooks. This is evident in the standardisation of car under-bodies while there has been the simultaneous development of the customisation of car upper-bodies to suit regional market needs (Miller 1994: 27).

The alliances that have occurred between auto companies in recent years have provided manufacturers with the opportunity for component and architecture sharing. For example, Fiat and GM have formed a joint venture to develop engines for both companies (Howell and Hsu 2002). The concept is to distribute, over a greater volume, the growing costs of designing the ever increasing number of models, the lifecycles of which are reduced due to the accelerated pace of product replacement (Freyssenet and Lung 2000). The platform strategy permits cost reduction to be reconciled with the greater variety that is required: the new products in the mature markets and the vehicles offered in emerging markets can be developed on the same platform. This essentially reduces design costs, R&D costs, lead time and increases economies of scale for shared components. In effect, this is a way to generate larger volumes from a single product development investment. The challenge, as noted by Howell and Hsu (2002) is to make the different models truly unique so that customers do not feel that their purchase is a 'look-alike' with another product.

Another important incentive in the establishment of automotive alliances is the need to reduce research and development costs. R&D is critical in the production process as manufacturers are under increasing pressure to provide more innovative products. Consumer demands, especially in mature markets, are increasing with respect to styling, quality, reliability and safety. At the same time, manufacturers face challenges on the energy and environmental front. While improvements can be made in the conventional engines in use today, manufacturers are looking ahead to hybrid vehicle technology, and ultimately to a hydrogen-based fuel-cell vehicle. The development costs and infrastructure required to create these developments are immense. Hence, there are significant gains to be made from alliances that share R&D and knowledge (Howell and Hsu 2002).

The changing relationship between auto assemblers and component manufacturers

As established markets matured, the search for new markets, to drive volume growth and balance risk, met with barriers to entry, which also prompted 'build where you sell' strategies. These have impacted upon both automobile manufacturers and the suppliers they required to co-locate to new assembly sites worldwide. Automobile production at the end of the century was structured upon a global network between the car assembler, suppliers, equipment producers, dealers and clients based on reciprocal interdependence (Calabrese 2001).

In many respects, the automobile industry is an example of a producer-driven supply chain. Historically, the leading assemblers in Western countries produced 60–70 per cent of the value of the vehicle in-house, and sourced most of the rest from component suppliers that were in a subordinate position (Humphrey 2000). The assemblers also controlled the design process, distribution (through dedicated dealers) and consumer finance. Some even organised the market in second-hand cars. However, this system is changing. The distribution system is now under challenge from independent dealers (particularly in North America), Western manufacturers have outsourced an increasing proportion of car production, leading suppliers have taken on a greater role in the design process and even some of the assemblers' design activities are being contracted out to independent design houses (Humphrey 2000).

When automobile manufacturers internationalised their operations between the 1950s and 1970s, they created new supplier networks at each new location (Humphrey 2000). In part, this was because they produced models particular to each market. However, when Ford began to produce identical vehicles at different locations in Europe in the 1970s, it combined central production of certain high-value products (engines, gearboxes etc.) with local supply networks for each plant. When the manufacturers expanded into emerging markets, they also created locally based networks. Within the context of trade protection, assemblers were often obliged to source a large part of their inputs from within the domestic economy. As such, the auto industry provided many opportunities for local companies, as long as they could compete on price and meet minimum quality standards.

In the past decade, however, these relationships have been transformed by the changing relationships between assemblers and first-tier suppliers in the global auto industry, and the increasingly global nature of the assembly and components industries. There has been a shift towards the supply of complete functions rather than individual components. A supplier will assemble parts into complete units (e.g. dashboards, body panels, seats etc.). In some cases, this involves the transfer of operations previously carried out in-house by the assembler. Also, with technological advances, systems are becoming more complex and as such the first-tier suppliers are becoming responsible for integration, leading to a greater role in managing the rest of the supply chain.

The shift away from self-contained supplier networks began in Europe in the 1970s. By using the same design and engineering for vehicles built in different countries, the advantages of using the same supplier for common parts became evident (Laigle 1995). Ideally, the assemblers would like to have the same part, with the same technology, the same quality system and the same underlying basis for inter-firm communication wherever they are making vehicles. Some components can be produced at centralised locations and shipped to widely spread assembly sites. However, logistics, costs and protectionism make local or regional production of many items a necessity (Humphrey 2000). For example, when the assemblers began investing in the emerging markets of Brazil, Argentina, China, ASEAN and India in the 1990s, the major components suppliers were pressured to follow their major customers. Assemblers and suppliers have thus developed parallel networks globally, and these are becoming increasingly important in the global auto industry.

As assemblers outsource more of their production and rely increasingly on their relationship with important component suppliers, the supply companies are growing in size, becoming multinational in outlook and are specialising in two or three key products (Saddler 1999). This trend is illustrated by the shift to modular assembly whereby the main component manufacturer not only supplies but also coordinates the design, manufacture and installation of the major parts or systems of the vehicle. Modular production is increasingly popular among American and European component makers.

In the past, a major justification for protecting the automotive industry was its supposed contribution to the development of national technological capabilities. The industry, even if dominated by large global manufacturers, would create opportunities for local companies in the components industry. However, the transformation of assembler–supplier relationships and the globalisation of design and production have led to considerable restructuring in the components industry. Mergers, acquisitions and the transfer of activities between companies have been evident. The components industry is becoming increasingly concentrated in companies that can design and provide systems and sub-assemblies across different markets.

The consequences of these trends have been clearly visible in new entrant countries such as India, South Africa and Brazil. For example, in Brazil, three of the four largest locally owned component manufacturers were sold to transnational companies between 1995 and 1997. In India, over the past decade, many new transnational companies have entered the market, and many local producers have been reduced to the status of second-tier suppliers.

By contrast with industries producing labour-intensive and standardised goods, production of automobiles makes relatively intensive use of human capital and is technologically advanced. Nonetheless, globalisation is also likely to have an impact on wages and employment in the auto industry. Trade models predict that the gains and costs of globalisation will be unevenly distributed among various employment groups and various sub-sectors of any industry, including automobile production. Low-skilled workers and labour intensive segments of the sectoral value chain in advanced industrialised economies are vulnerable to deteriorating wage and employment prospects because of competitive pressure from low-income countries (Spatz and Nunnenkamp 2002).

However, there is resistance from trade unions in various countries. Japanese auto makers such as Toyota, with their long histories of internalisation of production, are also hesitant about such developments. It remains to be seen whether modular production represents a fundamental shift or transformation in production. Some researchers think modular production is best suited to low-volume, small and niche market segments (Lung 2001).

Auto companies are now assuming more of an upstream global management and coordination role while outsourcing production and an increasing number of components. Some manufacturers are even withdrawing from areas that had long been deemed to be their core business, such as transmission and engine production. The shift to outsourcing may be an indication that auto companies are positioning themselves as future service providers. Lung (2001) suggests that an increasing number of auto firms are moving beyond a 'purely manufacturing-oriented perspective', which exclusively focuses on material production, to one that includes both material and immaterial aspects of automotive production. Any analysis of automobile production needs to encompass a production system that includes all sets of activities that interact closely with one another.

Almost every major auto manufacturer is now experimenting with downstream participation in one form or another, such as acquiring dealer networks, service and parts companies, ancillary products and telematics. Among some of the major companies there is evidence of a trend to reorient the auto industry from capital-intensive manufacturing to consumer-related activities. In 1999, Ford realigned much of its business towards consumer-related activities with higher potential for profits by purchasing Kwik-Fit, a tyre, exhaust and brake-fitting operation. Ford has also ventured into the internet, providing online build-to-order systems and its CEO, Jaques Nasser, announced his intention to position Ford as the leading auto company in e-commerce (Owen 2000). However, these developments preceded Nasser's dismissal by Ford which was in part due to problems associated with failures in these related companies, such as Firestone tyres, and Ford's subsequent reassessment of its global strategy (Table 2.3).

Location decisions and globalisation

The lean production debate has important implications for the future location strategies of the world auto industry as firms decide where to build new assembly plants and which existing plants to close down. Until the end of the 1960s, import substitution policies on the part of many countries (especially in developing economies) forced auto companies to establish plants locally in order to serve domestic markets. Depending upon regulations in the host country, production facilities ranged from simple assembly of pre-manufactured vehicle 'kits' to more

Table 2.3 Examples of downstream activities

Area	*Company*	*Example*
Vehicle insurance	Toyota	Investment in insurance company to develop Toyota-only car insurance in Japan
	BMW	Alliance with Chubb Group Insurance in the United States
Vehicle use activities	Honda, Jeep, Nissan, Toyota	High-speed and off-road test tracks; camps open to customers
Vehicle communication and emergency services	BMW	ASSIST Plus telematics service
	Daimler–Chrysler	Tegaron Telematics joint venture with Deutsche Telekom
	General Motors	GM OnStar telematics services
	Volkswagen	Gerdas telematics services (offered in Europe)
Vehicle repair activities	Renault	Joint venture with Autobacs Seven to set up an automotive accessories retail chain in Europe
Dealership investment	General Motors	Subsidiaries to begin investing in dealers in the US market
Certified used car programmes	Acura, BMW, Honda, General Motors, Lexus, Toyota	OEM certified used cars sold through dealers; some OEM's experiment with selling used cars directly over the internet

Source: Ealey and Troyano-Bermudez (2000).

Table 2.4 Trends in global production of automobiles by selected countries 2001–2007

Country	*2001*	*2003*	*2005*	*2007 (forecast)*	*Annualised growth rate (%)*
United States	11,224,640	11,853,598	12,276,113	12,167,696	1.50
Japan	9,133,594	9,313,570	9,243,208	9,178,101	0.24
Germany	5,061,417	4,958,394	5,133,812	5,161,791	0.05
China	1,900,106	3,422,338	5,017,792	6,182,145	33.34
South Korea	2,867,338	3,159,061	3,484,073	3,871,965	5.45
Brazil	1,706,673	1,697,429	1,999,508	2,196,195	4.87
India	728,255	855,972	1,102,315	1,212,243	10.48

Source: www.csmauto.com third quarter 2003 forecast.

complex operations. Australia was an example of a more advanced industrialised economy where tariff protection policies led to overseas auto firms establishing plants in order to gain access to a particular market, although these plants tended to be inefficient and uneconomical.

By the late 1980s it appeared that the globalisation of the automobile industry was leading to a multi-tiered system of vehicle manufacturing. Countries in the lowest tier of developing countries would produce simpler, less expensive components. More advanced developing countries (or newly industrialising economies) such as Mexico and Korea, which belonged to the second tier, would produce expensive entry-level cars and more complex components, using mass production techniques. The advanced industrialised countries in the top tier would produce the high value-added cars which were more technologically sophisticated and expensive using flexible or lean production techniques. As shown in Table 2.4, the largest growth rates in production up to the year 2007 are forecast to come from newer entry countries such as China, Thailand and Turkey although the largest auto producers continue to be the United States, Japan and Germany.

A number of factors effectively determine location decisions, but the transfer of production to low-cost locations has come at the expense of mature plants in North America and Western Europe. In order to protect their bottom line, some auto manufacturers have proven to be remarkably mobile. Until the mid-1990s, high levels of growth and low labour costs had encouraged Japanese firms to develop their activities with the ASEAN zone. However, by the time of the 1997 Asian economic crisis, declining sales encouraged Japanese firms to re-export their Southeast Asian production to other regions such as Latin America (Hatzfeld 1998). Diversification of production locations in different regions and strategies of multi-regionalism have largely protected manufacturers from regional economic cycles (Womack *et al.* 1990: 207).

Other important factors influencing location decisions include 'national issues' such as the economy and government of host nations, the transferability of global capital, the size of potential markets and the availability of a low-cost and quiescent workforce. Government regulations on imports and foreign investment also influence location decisions. For example, by directly investing public funds in joint ventures between transnational auto manufacturers and local companies, and restricting imports, governments may directly attract auto firms to move to new locations. On the other hand, auto firms are 'trapped' by protection policies, import duties and quotas into developing assembly operations in order to gain access to local markets, as was the case of Toyota in a number of Southeast Asian countries (Drury 2001).

As noted earlier, vehicle markets are predominantly regional rather than global. In extending their analysis of lean production to the global enterprise, Womack *et al.* (1990: 205) argued that for companies which sought to capture greater regional market share, there would be no substitute for production within the region. In the late 1990s, for example, Honda developed a set of products unique to, and produced within, each major region.

Establishing production centres based on regions carries a number of financial risks. These can be managed by limiting the sunk costs associated with investment so that a manufacturer is able to withdraw without suffering major financial damage should sales targets not be met. One method of controlling risks is to establish step by step systematic production in a new location. The auto assembler establishes a plant for complete knock down (CKD) or semi-knock down (SKD) vehicles and then transforms this into an assembly plant if sales reach projected levels. This strategy involves the risk that if sales boom, it may be impossible to catch up with competitors who established production facilities more quickly. Another strategy for limiting sunk costs is through sharing financial investment with a local producer. The sharing of financial resources offers advantages as the local partner has familiarity with the local economy (Lung 1998: 16–17). Other risks of exporting production to emerging countries include poorly developed infrastructures, inadequate road networks, well-developed used-car markets, the lack of conspicuous middle classes with associated purchasing power and mobility needs and the extremely low average income of the majority of the population in continental nations such as China and India.

It should not be assumed that the triad auto manufacturers are exporting solely to emerging regions. Global competition in the luxury market segment has encouraged specialist producers (e.g. BMW and Mercedes) to invest and produce in North America in order to counter penetration by Japanese competitors (Belis-Bergouignan *et al.* 1998). 'Global localism', whereby auto production is dispersed to developed countries alongside growing production among those countries themselves has given rise to three discernible trends (Deyo 1996: 9). First, an ensemble of countries is centred on regional integration. In North America for example, the big three are extending into Mexico, having invested in Canada. Second, there is peripheral regional integration like MERCOSUR and ASEAN. Third, there is an ensemble comprising South Korea, India and China. These countries have the economic means to develop an autonomous auto industry and because of the size of their potential markets, have considerable negotiation power with Eastern and Japanese carmakers (Freyssenet 1996: 5–6).

New competitors comprise end-producers and input suppliers from countries with relatively low per-capita income. In addition to developing and newly industrialising economies in Asia, Eastern and Central Europe as well as the so-called EU-periphery (Greece, Ireland, Portugal and Spain) belong to this income category. An analysis of the most important producers of automobiles among low-income countries reveals rising market shares especially for end producers located in Asia and in Southern and Central Europe. As a corollary, the share of the market by high-income industrial countries has continued to decline.

This shift in worldwide production of automobiles towards low-income countries only partly reflects increased competitive pressure from below. New suppliers such as China expanded the production of automobiles for serving protected local markets, while lacking international competitiveness. However, several new suppliers, including Mexico, South Korea and Spain, are increasingly successful in penetrating world automobile markets.

Although FDI has played a crucial role in its development, the automobile industry in emerging markets has developed under strikingly different conditions. In China, which opened up to FDI in the process of market-related reforms starting in the late 1970s, automobile production continues to be dominated by national companies. Korea set up an indigenous automobile industry (Daewoo/Ssangyong and Hyundai/Kia) which successfully penetrated world markets (see Chapters 2 and 3). In contrast to Mexico and Spain, Korea's exports of automobiles were not focused on neighbouring high-income countries, but were regionally diversified. As a consequence, traditional producers have been affected by competitive pressures from Korea both in their home markets and elsewhere, including the developing world. On the other hand, the development of an indigenous automobile industry rendered it more difficult for Korea to become integrated into global sourcing networks of automobile multinationals. Apart from assembling automobiles, locations such as Mexico, Spain and Central European countries in emerging economies have increasingly supplied traditional producer countries with automotive parts and components. In other words, competition from below goes beyond world-market oriented assembly operations in low-income countries and extends to imports of automotive inputs.

The evidence suggests that traditional automobile-producing countries will be subjected to increasing competitive pressure from new locations in low-income countries. Countries such as Mexico, Spain and the Czech Republic emerged as competitive suppliers of both finished automobiles and automotive parts. Other countries, notably Korea, have successfully focused on penetrating world markets for finished automobiles.

Conclusions

This chapter has outlined developments in the worldwide automotive industry and examined the factors which have promoted globalisation and limited the full realisation of the 'world car' concept. The stagnation of demand in mature markets and worldwide overcapacity in the industry has led manufacturers to develop a range of new strategies. On the demand side, there has been competition for shares in emerging markets to absorb existing products. On the supply side, manufacturers have sought to reduce costs, form alliances with other producers and create homogenous products to gain economies of scale. However, failure to achieve worldwide product strategies has led some companies to conclude that regional approaches may be more effective, especially in the high-volume market segment.

Led by Japanese companies, particularly Toyota, the mass production techniques pioneered by US auto companies have been strongly challenged by lean production. The latter involves continuous improvement in quality and productivity at all levels, close integration between production, component suppliers and customer service, as well as rapid product and process innovation. However, the process of moving from mass production to lean production is often incremental and there are various hybrid arrangements rather than a single approach to new forms of production combining elements of lean production with global competitive influences. In addition, the development of strategic alliances among some of the largest auto companies suggests the possibility of a new era of automotive production. This is illustrated by the trend among some companies to adopt 'techno-globalisation' which consists of global technology networks and technical alliances – particularly in relation to research and development.

Another trend has been towards global networks between car assemblers, suppliers, equipment producers, dealers and clients based on reciprocal interdependence. The transformation of assembler–supplier relationships has led to considerable restructuring of the components industry. Some auto-companies are assuming more of an upstream coordination role while outsourcing production and re-orienting their activities from capital-intensive manufacturing to consumer-related activities. However, the failure of the former CEO of Ford, Jacques Nasser, to reposition Ford as the 'leading auto company in e-commerce' and the subsequent reassessment by Ford of its global strategy calls into question some of the forecasts concerning the future of the industry.

The most important issue facing the industry is the long-term consequences of the decline of demand for automobile production in the mature economies, where most of the long-established companies are based, and the growth in the emerging markets. Many manufacturers have proven to be highly mobile but the transfer of production to low-cost locations has been at the expense of mature plants in North America and Western Europe and consequent job losses. Given the economic significance of the auto industry to many countries, and the concern of governments to both preserve existing plants and attract new investment by the industry, the future globalisation of the industry will depend on the interaction between the competitive strategies of firms and the roles played by governments around the world.

3 The Korean auto industry goes global

Introduction

Most traditional theories of foreign direct investment (FDI) do not deal with how firm-specific competitive (or ownership) advantage is created or augmented and are therefore limited in their ability to explain the emergence of latecomers, such as Korea, in international markets. Some theories begin by outlining the existing ownership advantages of a firm or they explain that firm-specific ownership advantages are developed internally through experience (Cantwell 1991). Others, such as Porter's *Diamond* (1990), list the conditions conducive to the creation of international competitive advantage. The experiences of Korean automobile companies do not fit neatly into these models. They did not have any substantial firm-specific ownership advantages when they started exporting in the international market in the early 1980s and most of the conditions in Porter's *Diamond* were not easily identifiable in the Korean automobile industry. Yet, the Korean auto industry has become one of the strongest competitors to the Japanese automobile companies.

This chapter examines the globalisation process of Korean manufacturing firms and, in particular, the Korean automobile industry. The section on globalisation of Korean manufacturing firms provides an overview of the globalisation strategies of the Korean manufacturing firms since the 1960s, with an emphasis on the revision of the strategy after the 1997 economic crisis. The next section surveys trends in FDI outflows from Korea since the mid-1980s and changes implemented after the economic crisis. The section after that briefly analyses the growth of the Korean automobile industry since its beginning in the early 1960s. The strategies for growth adopted by the Korean automobile industry are examined in the fifth section. The final section of the chapter discusses the international strategic alliances made by the Korean automobile companies and provides an analysis of their subsidiaries overseas.

Globalisation of Korean manufacturing firms

Most of the large Korean firms grew with a strong international orientation. From the beginning of industrialisation in the early 1960s, Korea's exports were the main engine of economic growth. As industrialisation proceeded, there has been a gradual shift of major export items during the 1960s, 1970s and 1980s. While labour-intensive goods enjoyed international competitiveness until the mid-1980s, capital and heavy industry goods emerged as new export items after the mid-1970s, supported by the aggressive export promotion policy of the Korean government. During the 1960s and 1970s, most of the globalisation process of Korean firms was confined to the expansion of export goods. Most of the subsidiaries established overseas during this period were representative offices and/or sales offices. Although the first FDI undertaken by Korean firms took place in 1968, FDI in the 1970s occurred only within natural resource development areas in order to support the expansion of heavy and chemical industries.

From the mid-1980s, Korean manufacturing companies began to consider other modes of servicing foreign markets. This was largely initiated by changes in their domestic and international business environments. In 1986, for the first time in the history of Korean industrialisation, the current account recorded massive surpluses. However, soaring wage rates and land prices sharply increased production costs and the problem was exacerbated by the appreciation of the Korean won.[1] Moreover, the massive current account surpluses created trade frictions with the major trading partners of the industrialised world.

When the Korean firms entered foreign markets, their generic strategy was mainly a 'low-cost' strategy to target the lower end of the market. As the competitiveness of traditional exports was eroded, Korean firms began to realign their strategy on three fronts. First, they sought to relocate their labour-intensive production processes overseas, in particular, Southeast Asia. Second, as traditional export items were subject to trade frictions and the movements towards North American Free Trade Agreement (NAFTA) and the European Union (EU) accelerated, they began to consider setting up production in closer proximity to these markets. Finally, they attempted to upgrade their major export items to capital and technology-intensive products. In order to compete with exports from Southeast Asia and China, they were forced to upgrade the quality of their products. For this, however, they could not continue to rely merely on borrowed technology and 'reverse engineering'.

Hence, there was an urgent need to develop and acquire new technology. These three motives caused the Korean firms to realign globalisation policies, resulting in a rapid expansion of FDI in the 1990s.[2] While the size of the companies and the quantity of their international transactions increased significantly during the 1990s, their brand names were beginning to be better recognised in international markets. Yet, in many cases, this international expansion was an extension of domestic strategy, focusing on the market size and power rather than relying on the internal core competence. As oligopolistic competition in the domestic market intensified, many firms looked to explore opportunities overseas and undertake FDI, following other firms which entered the foreign market.[3]

This active globalisation of Korean firms reversed its course dramatically in the wake of the Asian financial crisis in 1997. The Korean economy was severely affected by the crisis when its banking system was unable to pay its large international debt or maintain the stability of the currency. The roots of this crisis were in the close relationship between the large Korean conglomerates and the state-controlled banking sector which was created to assist rapid industrialisation of Korean economy from the 1960s. However, this relationship resulted in widespread corruption and provided the conglomerates with ready access to state support in times of crisis. Hence, the Korean conglomerates were able to achieve their rapid growth in size, financed through large borrowings. Over time, the level of insolvent debts held by Korean banks and the large corporations increased considerably. When the instability of the financial crisis struck the Korean economy in late 1997, the collapse of the currency increased the level of international debt to the extent that many large firms and banks were unable to meet their repayments.[4] For example, the average debt/equity ratio of the top 30 conglomerates (excluding the finance and banking sector) had reached 450 per cent by December 1997. The sharp depreciation of the Korean won meant that the debt/equity ratio doubled between 1996 and 1997.[5] Therefore, the short-term mobility of funds during the 1997 crisis was only a symptom of the problem, whereas more fundamental causes were among their business practices and the economic policies of the state.

This financial crisis instigated massive reform of the state's economic policies and expansion strategies of Korean firms. The state was no longer the supporting agent for the large conglomerates to secure large loans and expand into new areas of business. Some conglomerates, such as Daewoo Business Group, that were unable to sustain their operations due to large debts, faced bankruptcy. Others undertook serious restructuring in order to survive. The restructuring forced by the 1997 economic crisis covered almost all facets of Korean business practices. Large Korean conglomerates dramatically downsized their operations and revised their debt- and volume-based growth strategy, known as an 'Octopus Arm' style (Kwon and Suh 2003). To address insolvency, firms were forced to attract foreign capital either by selling off their unrelated businesses in Korea or those overseas. In some business groups, this restructuring meant a significant reduction of the member companies, while the rest of the companies were sold off. However, other business groups, such as the Hyundai group, were divided into several smaller groups to increase efficiency and profitability.

For the first time since the creation of the *chaebol*, operational efficiency and profitability were placed as priorities ahead of market share and the size of the company. All new investments, including FDI, needed careful scrutiny in terms of their profitability. These initiated two significant changes in the foreign subsidiaries of the Korean companies. First, inefficient foreign subsidiaries were sold off to ease the pressures to finance the debt (Kwon *et al.* 2004). Second, foreign subsidiaries began to consider themselves more as independent business units in terms of profitability, rather than mere service units of the parent company. Hence, in addition to the rationalisation of the *chaebol* groups, the globalisation strategies of the Korean companies began to be fine tuned after the 1997 economic crisis.

Trends in FDI outflows and the 1997 economic crisis

The globalisation process of an industry can be examined broadly from two perspectives. First, investigating the changes in the mode of servicing the foreign markets such as export, licensing, franchising and direct investment; and second, the relationship between firms, including the intra-firm relationship such as the headquarter–subsidiary relationships and the inter-firm relationships such as strategic alliances and global supply chains. In the process of industrialisation, the Korean government did not encourage inward FDI until the late 1990s, relying on loans to finance the investment needed. Consequently, the degree of interdependence between domestic and foreign firms has been much lower than that in many other countries. For technology development, Korean firms followed the Japanese model, relying more on purchased technology and reverse engineering than on technical alliances.

As mentioned in the previous section, FDI has been a rather recent phenomenon in Korea and until recently FDI outflows have been more active than inflows. Before examining the globalisation process of the Korean automobile industry, the trends of FDI outflows from Korea, and the impact of the economic crisis on FDI will be surveyed.

Table 3.1 shows the trends in FDI outflows from Korea since the mid-1980s. During the period from 1986 to 1990, the volume of FDI increased by 74 per cent per annum. After a decrease in the early 1990s, the growth rate recovered in the mid-1990s. The cumulative stock of FDI by Korean firms reached US$13.7 million in 1996, approximately six times that of 1990. However, the trends changed substantially in the late 1990s. As shown in Table 3.1, this growth of FDI halted in the late 1990s due to the 1997 economic crisis and has tended to fluctuate since. The average size of FDI increased in 1993, reached a peak in 1998 and then decreased substantially. Two reasons can be found for this. First, since the 1997 crisis, the Korean *chaebols* have revised their strategy by placing more emphasis on efficiency rather than simply increasing the size of the company. Consequently, *chaebols* have been more careful in making large investments overseas. Second, although the relative capacity of small- and medium-sized firms to engage in FDI deteriorated after the crisis, this situation is gradually improving.

As shown in Table 3.1, the 1990s saw the manufacturing sector, especially electronics and automobiles, overtake the mining industry as the main investor. Table 3.1 shows that FDI by the manufacturing sector increased from US$603 million in 1991, to US$1,486 million in 1994 and US$2,232 million in 1996. However, manufacturing was the Korean sector most affected by the financial crisis of 1997. Table 3.1 reveals a decreasing trend after the 1997 economic crisis until 2000, reaching the pre-crisis level only in 2001.

Table 3.2 shows trends of FDI outflows from Korea by major host regions. In the 1980s, most of the FDI to the United States was designed to facilitate and assist direct exports from Korea, whereas FDI to Southeast Asia represented the relocation of manufacturing plants, which were losing their competitiveness in Korea. The direction of FDI to less-developed countries (LDCs) and

Table 3.1 Trends in total FDI outflow from Korea

Year	*Agriculture and fishing*	*Mining*	*Manufacturing*	*Construction*	*Trade and retail*	*Transport and warehousing*	*Telecommunication*	*Financing and insurance*	*Hotels and restaurants*	*Real estate and services*	*Others*	*Total (A)*	*Number of projects (B)*	*Average size (A/B)*
1986	4	83	77	2	16	0	0	0	0	1	0	183	50	3.7
1987	6	219	157	3	23	1	0	0	1	1	0	411	91	4.5
1988	15	65	85	5	39	1	0	1	1	4	0	216	172	1.3
1989	74	76	280	13	63	2	0	0	50	14	0	572	270	2.1
1990	41	152	485	5	229	2	0	0	24	21	0	959	340	2.8
1991	17	123	606	13	228	10	0	0	66	53	0	1,116	445	2.5
1992	24	150	657	1	304	11	3	0	48	21	0	1,219	497	2.5
1993	13	146	560	20	444	6	1	0	65	8	0	1,263	688	1.8
1994	14	115	1,489	31	553	14	8	0	44	34	0	2,302	1,488	1.5
1995	23	77	2,021	80	320	43	296	0	56	187	0	3,103	1,322	2.3
1996	21	249	2,791	87	613	25	165	0	109	254	0	4,314	1,463	2.9
1997	17	213	1,756	83	486	28	420	0	190	334	0	3,527	1,316	2.7
1998	17	104	1,977	88	1,737	10	117	0	10	158	0	4,218	607	7
1999	8	121	1,483	44	784	53	34	2	61	150	0	2,740	1,078	2.5
2000	18	40	1,231	49	569	11	94	9	22	1,881	2	3,926	2,024	1.9
2001	*8*	*46*	*2,568*	*23*	*343*	*9*	*38*	*2*	*26*	*196*	*0*	*3,259*	*2,032*	*1.6*

Source: The Korea Federation of Banks (2002), *Overseas Direct Investment Statistics Yearbook*, The Korea Federation of Banks, Seoul.

Note
Unit: project, US$1 million.

Table 3.2 FDI trends by major host regions

Year	*Southeast Asia*			*North America*			*Europe*		
	No. of projects	*Amount*	*(%)*	*No. of projects*	*Amount*	*(%)*	*No. of projects*	*Amount*	*(%)*
1986	12	4	2	27	81	44	3	6	3
1987	18	132	31	41	189	46	10	7	2
1988	66	45	21	57	96	44	16	15	7
1989	125	128	22	74	285	50	16	19	3
1990	185	290	30	86	438	46	21	64	7
1991	270	426	38	83	460	41	35	89	8
1992	360	521	43	61	391	32	33	143	12
1993	553	504	40	58	390	31	32	175	14
1994	1,214	1,152	50	135	567	25	55	357	16
1995	1,038	1,731	56	137	550	18	70	590	19
1996	1,073	1,773	41	198	1,562	36	72	604	14
1997	906	1,693	48	227	883	25	71	374	11
1998	392	1,705	40	135	898	21	38	1,143	27
1999	663	1,082	40	319	1,113	41	40	295	11
2000	1,149	995	25	699	1,217	31	65	150	4
2001	1,356	968	30	506	414	13	66	1,751	54

Source: The Korea Federation of Banks (2002), *Overseas Direct Investment Statistics Yearbook*, The Korea Federation of Banks, Seoul.

Notes
These three regions account for 85 per cent of FDI outflows from Korea. Southeast Asia includes China.
Unit: project, US$1 million.

developed countries (DCs) changed considerably from the late 1990s onwards. LDCs in Southeast Asia, as destinations for FDI by Korean firms, lost their relative importance, whereas FDI by Korean firms into DCs increased. As shown in Table 3.2, of the total amount invested (US$3,105 million) in 1995, 56 per cent was invested in the Southeast Asia region but declined to 38 per cent (US$4,219 million) in 1998, decreasing further to 30 per cent in 2001. By contrast, 37 per cent of the total FDI went to DCs in 1995, reaching 67 per cent in 2001.

In all regions, the negative impacts of the 1997 financial crisis were reflected as significant fluctuations in FDI outflows. FDI to the United States increased significantly in 1998 but has been decreasing rapidly since then, whereas FDI to the European Union has shown a marked revival in 2001. FDI to Southeast Asia has been decreasing continuously since the crisis, although its share in total investment recovered slightly in 2001. However, the average size of FDI to Southeast Asia has been decreasing, while the number of projects has been increasing since the crisis. This implies that Southeast Asia, including China, is still the most popular destination for FDI by small- and medium-size industry.

In the second half of the 1990s, Korean firms expanded their globalisation strategies to include subsidiary companies in a more diverse range of countries. Several factors could be driving this trend. Until the end of the 1980s, most subsidiaries of Korean companies in advanced countries were either sales offices or representative offices, that is, market-oriented investment. However, since the mid-1990s, a new motivation has emerged for investment in DCs, namely, to acquire technology. Traditionally, the Korean government did not encourage inward FDI for the country's industrial development. Most of Korean firms developed their technologies through licensing, purchasing and reverse engineering. However, as the Korean wage bill increased and the traditional industries were losing their competitive advantage, the old ways of technology acquisition were neither appropriate nor sufficient. While increasing their internal R&D budgets significantly, large Korean firms established subsidiaries in the advanced countries to acquire technology.

In the 1980s, trade-oriented investment in Asia was motivated by cheap labour. However, there have been significant changes in the 1990s (Suh and Seo 1999). As the standard of living increased in East and Southeast Asia, the region became important as a market destination. The recessions in the Japanese domestic economy, the continued growth in China and the prospect of ASEAN economies becoming a single large market reinforced this trend. On the other hand, many companies had already relocated their labour-intensive production processes to Southeast Asia. As a result, relocation of labour-intensive industries was gradually losing its importance as a major reason for investing in Southeast Asia. Hence, although FDI in East and Southeast Asia since the 1990s remains a combination of both market and trade-oriented investment, the former is becoming more important (Suh and Seo 1999).

Table 3.3 traces the trends in the manufacturing FDI outflows from Korea according to industries. As shown in Table 3.3, FDI in the declining industries such as textile and footwear increased only marginally in the early 1990s and

Table 3.3 FDI outflow in the Korean manufacturing sector

Type	*1985*		*1992*		*1994*		*1995*		*1996*		*1997*		*1998*	
Food and beverages	5.0	(5.4)	123.1	(5.4)	166.3	(4.0)	231.3	(3.8)	350.4	(4.5)	379.8	(4.4)	413.8	(3.9)
Textile and clothes	3.4	(3.7)	310.6	(13.7)	545.5	(13.0)	730	(12.1)	949.2	(12.3)	1,075.4	(12.3)	1158.4	(10.9)
Leather and footware	2.3	(2.5)	90.3	(4.0)	210.1	(5.0)	271.8	(4.5)	321.9	(4.2)	345.1	(4.0)	356.3	(3.4)
Wood and furniture	6.9	(7.4)	94.3	(4.1)	117.4	(2.8)	150.2	(2.5)	160.3	(2.1)	171.1	(2.0)	183.3	(1.7)
Paper and printing	1.4	(1.5)	49.4	(2.2)	86.1	(2.1)	95.9	(1.6)	126.9	(1.6)	168.1	(1.9)	176.8	(1.7)
Petroleum and chemical	18.5	(19.9)	264.5	(11.6)	408.1	(9.7)	531.9	(8.8)	657.9	(8.5)	729.7	(8.4)	886.5	(8.4)
Non-metallic mineral	29.3	(8.0)	117.4	(5.2)	231.5	(5.5)	365.1	(6.1)	397.9	(5.2)	386.6	(4.4)	343.4	(3.2)
Basic metals	4.5	(4.8)	399	(17.5)	464.4	(11.1)	545.9	(9.1)	703.1	(9.1)	913.4	(10.5)	967.8	(9.1)
Fabricated metals, machinery and equipment	15.7	(16.9)	667.2	(29.3)	1,627.4	(38.8)	2,660.3	(44.2)	3,466.6	(44.9)	3,892.5	(44.6)	5,296.7	(49.9)
Others	5.8	(6.3)	157.9	(6.9)	334.3	(8.0)	430.4	(7.2)	589.1	(7.6)	660	(7.6)	816.3	(7.7)
Total	92.8	(100.0)	2,273.7	(100.0)	4,191.1	(100.0)	6,012.8	(100.0)	7,723.3	(100.0)	8,721.7	(100.0)	10,599.3	(100.0)

Source: The Korea Federation of Banks (1998, 1999), *Overseas Direct Investment Statistics Yearbook*, The Korea Federation of Banks, Seoul.; The Bank of Korea (1997), *Overseas Direct Investment Statistics Yearbook*, The Bank of Korea, Seoul.

Note
Unit: US$1 million (%).

its/their relative importance decreased in the late 1990s. In contrast, FDI in fabricated metals, machinery and equipment sectors have grown rapidly since the early 1990s. In particular, its annual growth ratio reached over 39 per cent between 1994 and 1998, accounting for 50 per cent of total manufacturing FDI outflows in 1998. Among these sectors, FDI from the electronics industry was the most active, accounting for more than 70 per cent of the FDI in fabricated metals. As is the case with other industries, there are two types of FDI undertaken by the Korean electronics industry. One is to relocate low-quality and low value-added electronics products into LDCs, for example, old model domestic appliances and low-quality computer chips for which low production cost are some of the most important factors for international competitiveness. Another important factor is the development of high-quality and high value-added electronics products utilising sophisticated technologies and high-quality labours such as digital TV sets, semiconductors, advanced computer hardware and software. As the size of the investment needed is much larger in the automobile industry compared with the electronics industry, relocation of production facilities in the automobile industry took place at a much slower pace.

Growth of the Korean automobile industry

Our previous analysis of globalisation strategies of large Korean companies and trends of outward FDI has revealed that many Korean firms have become major global players within the first 30 years of their life. As is the case with many other manufacturing companies, the Korean automobile industry has a relatively brief history. This history will be followed by an analysis of the process of globalisation.

The Korean automobile industry began as a repair industry for the vehicles released during and after the Korean War. The first assembly plant was established in 1955 with an annual capacity of 1,500 units. When the Korean government launched the first Five-Year Economic Development Plan in 1962, it introduced the Automobile Industry Protection Law and began to promote the automobile industry. The development of the Korean automobile industry since 1962 can be divided into three periods: the preparation for local production (1962–1971), development of Korean models (1972–1982) and the period of mass production and globalisation (1983–present) (Hyun 1991: 62–67).

During the first period (1962–1971), Saenara Motor Company was established through a technical alliance with Nissan in 1962. However, due to the shortage of foreign exchange, the company went bankrupt and was taken over by Shinjin Motor company, which had a technical alliance with Toyota. Shinjin produced *Corona* as a Complete Knock-Down (CKD) production. During this period, Kia Motors began assembling small trucks, and Hadongwhan Motor Co. began assembling buses.

Hyundai Motor Company (hereafter Hyundai) and Asia Motors (hereafter Asia) were the next to be established. Hyundai began producing *Cortina* in 1968 through a technical alliance with Ford, while Asia produced *Fiat 124*, with a technical alliance with Fiat. The government announced a localisation plan in 1970, planning to increase the localisation ratio from 38 per cent in 1970 100 per cent for small passenger cars by 1972, and for all cars by 1974. However, the localisation rate achieved by the end of 1972 was only 50 per cent.

The Korean automobile industry grew very rapidly during the second period (1972–1982). The government announced 'A Long-term Plan to Promote the Automobile Industry' in 1974, which consisted of three major targets: to achieve a localisation ratio of 85 per cent by 1975, see that 80 per cent of domestic sales were to be in the small car segments below the engine capacity of 1500cc and to achieve an export target of 75,000 units by 1981. As Toyota divested from Korea in the mid-1970s, Shinjin Motors established General Motors Korea, a joint venture with General Motors (GM), which was subsequently purchased by Daewoo. After Asia was taken over by Kia, the Korean automobile industry had a triad of producers: Hyundai, Kia and Daewoo. Hyundai developed its own model *Pony*, while Kia and GMK produced *Brisa* and *Gemini* respectively. By 1976, three companies had achieved a localisation ratio of 85 per cent.

The global recessions, which began in late 1979, resulted in severe excess capacities in the Korean automobile industry. The Korean government therefore announced a plan to consolidate the automobile industry in Korea in August 1980. The details of the plan were only confirmed in July 1982. First, the small passenger cars were to be produced only by Hyundai and Saehan (Daewoo). Second, Kia was to concentrate on small to medium commercial vehicles. Third, buses and large trucks were opened to competition. Although these measures were adopted in order to avoid creating excessive competition and excess capacities, they resulted in a substantial contraction of the industry. Table 3.4 shows the production and export data for the Korean automobile industry since 1976. The consequences of the decree in the early 1980s are shown in Table 3.4. The automobile production decreased only in the year 1980 in the history of the Korean automobile production. This decrease was different from the temporary reduction in 1988 after the economic crisis. It took until 1983 for the level of production to return to the 1979 level.

The Korean automobile industry began exporting in 1976, starting with South America. However, the major expansion in export during this period was into the European Community (EC) market. By 1982, exports to EC accounted for 52 per cent of total automobile exports. During this period, the Korean automobile industry 'took off' as one of the major industries in Korea, while achieving a localisation ratio of 90 per cent by 1981.

The third period, which began in 1983, can be characterised as *a period of mass production*. In 1985, Hyundai Motors built a production plant with an annual capacity of 300,000 units, while Daewoo built a plant with an annual production capacity of 170,000 units. After the restrictions on the production of small passenger cars were lifted in 1987, Kia developed its own model *Pride* and expanded its production capacity to 120,000 units.

As the domestic markets were saturated with the rapid increase in production capacity, the three companies began exploring the international market aggressively. By the mid-1980s, more than 50 per cent of total production was

Table 3.4 Korean automobile production and exports

Year	*Production (A)*	*Domestic sales (%)*		*Export (%)*	
1976	49,549	48,306	(97.5)	1,243	(2.5)
1977	85,210	76,074	(89.3)	9,136	(10.7)
1978	158,958	132,621	(83.4)	26,337	(16.6)
1979	204,447	172,861	(84.6)	31,486	(15.4)
1980	123,135	97,883	(79.5)	25,252	(20.5)
1981	133,084	108,147	(81.3)	24,937	(18.7)
1982	162,590	141,988	(87.4)	20,602	(12.6)
1983	221,019	195,663	(88.7)	25,356	(11.3)
1984	265,361	213,011	(80.4)	52,350	(19.6)
1985	378,162	255,052	(53.5)	123,110	(46.5)
1986	601,546	295,177	(49.1)	306,369	(50.9)
1987	979,739	433,429	(44.2)	546,310	(55.8)
1988	1,083,655	507,521	(46.9)	576,134	(53.1)
1989	1,129,470	773,430	(68.5)	356,040	(31.5)
1990	1,321,630	974,530	(73.8)	347,100	(26.2)
1991	1,497,818	1,107,456	(73.9)	390,362	(26.1)
1992	1,729,696	1,273,541	(73.6)	456,155	(26.4)
1993	2,050,208	1,411,651	(68.9)	638,557	(31.1)
1994	2,311,663	1,573,720	(68.2)	737,943	(31.8)
1995	2,526,400	1,547,712	(61.3)	978,688	(38.7)
1996	2,812,714	1,602,557	(57.0)	1,210,157	(43.0)
1997	2,818,275	1,501,384	(53.4)	1,316,891	(46.6)
1998	1,954,494	592,330	(31.0)	1,362,164	(69.0)
1999	2,843,114	1,333,454	(47.0)	1,509,660	(53.0)
2000	3,114,998	1,438,556	(46.2)	1,676,442	(53.8)
2001	2,946,329	1,445,116	(49.1)	1,501,213	(50.9)

Source: Korea Automobile Manufacturers Association, Korean Automobile Industry, 1976–2001.

exported and the Korean automobile industry became one of the major exporting industries in Korea.[6] As the Korean economy continued to record huge current account surpluses for four consecutive years from 1986 to 1989, trading partners in the industrialised world began to put pressure on Korean exports, which contributed to a substantial decrease in exports after 1989. During the period of sluggish exports from 1989 to 1993, domestic consumption continued to expand and more than offset the decline in exports. This provided a buffer for the fluctuations in export demand until the mid-1990s. Since the mid-1990s, however, exports have again accounted for more than 50 per cent of the total production.

Entering at the lower end and moving up

The previous section surveyed the growth path of the Korean automobile industry, which started with the domestic sales but was soon able to compete in the international market. The industry's dependence on the expansion of international sales became evident in the 1980s. However, operating in the international automobile market has not been easy. Many companies enjoy good reputations, which makes it very difficult for new entrants to penetrate the market. Japanese companies had already obtained global recognition with high quality and reasonable prices, which called for strong competition in nearly every segment of the international automobile market. Moreover, the global automobile industry had generally been suffering from excess capacity in the 1990s. In this unfavourable international environment, how did the Korean companies manage to grow? What factors contributed to such a remarkable performance?

The first factor that can be singled out is the relentless support from the government. From 1962, the Korean government had a vision to create the automobile industry. The government provided the industry with protection from the competition of imports and guided the industry through various plans, regulations and decrees. This is one explanation of the rapid expansion of the domestic sales. However, protection against imports cannot explain the rapid expansion of exports. It was the expansionist spirit of the Korean *chaebols* and accompanying massive investments that enabled the industry to enjoy economies of scale and reduce costs. In fact, the size of the investment was so huge, that the industry would have faced bankruptcy if it had not exported. As explained before, the end of the 1970s was a very difficult period for the Korean automobile industry, due to the global recession. However, in the mid-1980s, all three companies made huge investments. The third factor can be found in the aggressive export-oriented strategy adopted by the Korean companies. Competition in the export market prevented Korean companies from becoming complacent under the government's protectionist policies. The fourth factor is the motivated and diligent workforce which gave the Korean automobile industry a distinct competitive edge.

Porter's *Diamond* (1990) explains the international competitiveness of an industry in terms of the environmental factors in the home country. Although this view has been discredited by many scholars in international business as inadequate explanations of the source of a firm's international competitiveness, a careful examination reveals that it is still relevant in the case of the Korean automobile industry, especially in the first stage of its globalisation. The major sources of its competitiveness can be found in environmental factors such as government policy and an efficient and well-trained labour force. The only factor that was specific to the Korean automobile industry was the vision and leadership of senior executives, more specifically those of the CEO's, which motivated their employees.

There are similarities and differences between the globalisation of the Japanese and Korean auto companies. In assessing how the Korean automobile industry managed to create core competence, it is useful to compare the two countries' experiences, especially from the early to mid-1990s.

Table 3.5 shows a comparison of production and sales by the Korean and Japanese automobile companies from the early to mid-1990s. In 1992, the size of the domestic market in Japan was five times larger than that in Korea. Although

Table 3.5 A comparison of production and sales by the Korean and Japanese automobile companies

		1992	*1993*	*1994*	*1995*
Korea	Overseas production	40 (3%)[a]	64 (3%)	49 (3%)	105 (4%)
	Domestic production				
	Total	1,730 (97%)[a]	2,050 (97%)	2,311 (97%)	2,526 (96%)
	(Domestic sales)	1,273 (73%)[b]	1,411 (70%)	1,573 (67%)	1,547 (61%)
	(Export)	457 (27%)[b]	639 (30%)	738 (33%)	979 (39%)
Japan	Overseas production	4,093 (25%)[a]	4,608 (29%)	5,198 (33%)	5,622 (35%)
	Domestic production				
	Total	12,627 (75%)[a]	11,485 (71%)	10,987 (67%)	10,656 (65%)
	(Domestic sales)	6,959 (55%)[b]	6,467 (56%)	6,527 (59%)	6,865 (64%)
	(Export)	5,668 (45%)[b]	5,018 (44%)	4,460 (41%)	3,791 (36%)

Source: Song, 1998, pp. 177–178.

Notes
a Share in the total production.
b Share in the domestic production.

Toyota started exporting to the US market in the 1950s, the major momentum for growth of the Japanese automobile industry during the 1950s and 1960s came from the sales in the domestic market (Moon 1995: 110–113). After the domestic demand had achieved a stable growth, the Japanese automobile industry expanded very rapidly during the 1970s and overseas production started in the early 1980s.

However, by the early 1990s, the Japanese automobile industry had already begun its restructuring in response to the increase in wages and appreciation of the Japanese Yen. The deep recession in the 1990s encouraged Japanese auto companies to relocate more of their production overseas. As a result, both the domestic production and direct exports from Japan decreased substantially in the first half of the 1990s. By 1995 Japanese companies accounted for about 35 per cent of the global production through their subsidiaries outside Japan. Meanwhile, the globalisation strategy of Japanese auto companies focused on the expansion of the overseas production and coordination of parts supplies among various global production centres (Song 1998: 176–180). As they relocated their production bases to the United States after the sharp appreciation of the Japanese yen, Japanese auto companies regained their market share in the United States by the mid-1990s.[7]

By 1995, the proportion of exports to total domestic production in Korea was similar to that of Japan. This was a significant achievement for a latecomer in the international market. Yet, the globalisation strategy of the Korean automobile industry was still focused mainly on exporting domestically produced cars until the mid-1990s. While in Japan domestic sales were stagnant and exports were decreasing, both the domestic sales and the exports grew simultaneously in Korea. Although overseas production by Korean auto companies had begun to increase in the late 1990s, the proportion of overseas production remained very small and most of the production continued to take place in Korea.

The increase in the production capacity of Korean auto producers during the 1990s could not be absorbed solely by domestic sales. Hence, the expansion of exports was necessary to achieve not only economies of scale but also to avoid excess capacities in the domestic market. This became not just a priority but also the only means for survival. The Korean automobile industry therefore tried hard to expand its global market share. The composition of investment budgets supports this trend. In the early 1990s, approximately 65 per cent of the investment budget in Japan was spent on the R&D investment, whereas 70 per cent of the investment budget in the Korean automobile industry was spent on the facility investment. The total investment budget in Korea was 50 per cent larger than in Japan (Song 1998: 179–180). This indicates that the Korean automobile industry's globalisation strategy began before acquiring substantial firm-specific competitive advantage. By contrast, the Japanese firms' globalisation strategy was based on distinct firm-specific competitive advantage which was developed through experiences in domestic production.

The Korean automobile industry, in the early 1990s, was rapidly catching up to the Japanese industry in terms of production capacity, quality and globalisation strategy. Like most of the Korean manufacturing sector, the automobile industry adopted the Japanese strategy to 'enter at the lower end and move upward'. In the first stage of international market expansion, this strategy was largely based on price competition. However, a lack of established firm-specific advantages meant that this was a very demanding task for Korean auto companies. Cost reduction was the main priority and gaining a secure market share was considered much more important than creating short-term profit. This strategy may not have been sustainable by the Korean firms in the medium to long run if it had not been for a long planning horizon and aggressive expansionist strategy in Korea, combined with strong visions of the CEOs of the companies.

Table 3.6 shows a comparison of the number of defects in cars sold in the US market in the early 1990s, which can be used as a proxy for quality indicators. As shown in Table 3.6, there were differences in quality between the companies. The competitive advantage of the Korean cars in the early 1990s was based on lower prices.

However, Table 3.6 also indicates that there has been a continuous improvement in quality in order to achieve global competitiveness. Table 3.7 shows a comparison of average assembly time per vehicle in the early 1990s. As shown in the Table 3.7, the average assembly time per vehicle in Korea was nearly twice as long as that in Japan. A comparison of productivity indicators among parts suppliers in the United States, Japan and Korea, shown in Table 3.8, indicates a similar trend. The production processes of the parts suppliers in Korea were a lot more labour intensive than their counterparts in the United States and Japan. The fact that Korean cars were still competing in the low-price segments of the market implies that both wage rates and labour productivity were critical factors in

Table 3.6 Comparison of the number of defects (number of defects during the first 90 days among 100 new vehicles)

Year	*United States*		*Japan*		*Korea*	*Germany*	*Average*
	GM	*Ford*	*Toyota*	*Honda*	*Hyundai*	*Mercedes*	
1989	169	149	117	113	178	103	148
1991	134	127	90	111	235	99	133
1992	136	129	83	106	193	NA	125
1993	95	112	74	92	194	95	107

Source: Moon (1995: 96).

Table 3.7 A comparison of average assembly time per vehicle in Korea, Japan, the United States and Europe

Year	*Korea*	*United States*	*Japan*	*Europe*
1990	32.5	25.1	16.8	35.6
1993	26.5	20.6	16.8	26.7

Source: Moon (1995: 96).

Table 3.8 A comparison of productivity indicators among the automobile part suppliers in 1995 (United States, Japan and Korea)

Productivity indicators	*Korea*	*Japan*	*United States*
Number of machines per worker	1.4	7.4	2.5
Time taken to change dies on the pressing machine (minutes)	48.0	7.9	114.3
Amount of inventories (days)	8.0	1.5	8.1

Source: Kim (1995: 36).

determining the competitiveness of Korean exports. This supports the argument that human resource management was one of the critical sources of the Korean companies' competitiveness, as human resource management played a key role by managing the workforce in these labour intensive production systems.

As mentioned before, an examination of the growth of the Korean automobile industry in the 1990s confirmed that it began globalisation before developing significant firm-specific competitive advantages. Consequently, it had to compete in terms of price in the lower segments of the market, which had been vacated by the Japanese automobile companies. However, it should be noted that only some factors in Porter's *Diamond* are relevant, as the size and the quality of the domestic market were not conducive to the creation of the international firm-specific competitive advantages.

Porter (1990) also identified the change in the source of competitiveness and the momentum for a firm's growth. In the first phase, the sources of competitiveness can be found in the resources used in the production, whereas in the second phase the growth is driven by investment. In the third phase, it is led by technology development and in the last stage it becomes stagnant. This is a relevant explanation of the Korean automobile industry's growth pattern. During the 1990s, huge investment in the Korean auto industry certainly provided the momentum for growth and assisted the industry to develop and sustain price competitiveness.

As noted before, one of the important differences between the Korean and Japanese automobile industries was the role of the domestic market. By and large, the Japanese auto industry developed its technological and managerial competence in domestic production. Firm-specific competitive advantages developed in domestic production enabled the Japanese automobile industry to compete in the international market in the 1990s. However, as the Korean automobile industry entered the international markets before developing its firm-specific competitive advantages, the international experience of the Korean automobile industry in the 1990s assisted it to develop and accumulate its competitive advantages. For example, competition in the US market was one of the important factors that drove the improvement in product quality.

Like the duration of the globalisation process, Korea and Japan differed in their approach to globalisation. The Japanese path can be summarised as 'Import Substitution → Stable Growth based on Domestic Demand → Exports to LDCs → Exports to DCs → Production in LDCs → Production in DCs' (Moon 1995). However, the Korean path can be summarised as 'Import Substitution → Rapid Growth of Industry simultaneously with Increase in Exports to DCs → Exports to LDCs → Production in LDCs → Production in DCs.'[8]

This meant that the Korean automobile companies exported to the EC and US market before they expanded their sales to less-developed countries.[9] The US and EC markets were large enough to warrant rapid growth of exports, and the success in the US market would facilitate Korean companies' expansion into other markets. Although it is much more difficult to export to the US market without substantial experience in exporting to the markets of less-developed countries, this can shorten the process of gaining secure market shares in the international markets, and the time to gain global recognition.

Figure 3.1 and Table 3.9 show the composition of automobile exports from Korea by destination. While the exports before 1985 were mainly to the EC, the US market became the major destination of the Korean automobile exports during the rest of the 1980s. As the trade frictions intensified and the Japanese companies regained their competitiveness in the US market, the Korean automobile companies tried to diversify their export markets to include LDCs in

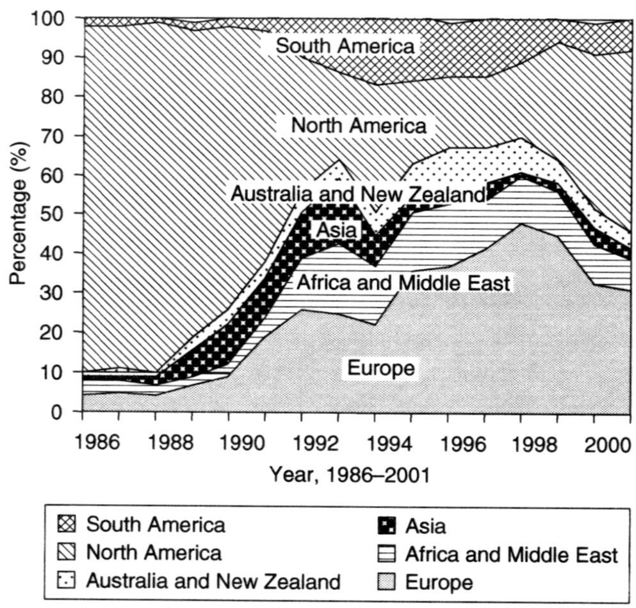

Figure 3.1 Korean automobile exports by destination.

Source: Korea Automobile Manufacturers Association, Korean Automobile Industry, 1998–2002.

Table 3.9 Automobile exports from Korea by destination

Year	*Europe*	*North America*	*South America*	*Africa and Middle East*	*Asia*	*Pacific (Australia and NZ)*	*Total*
1986	12,131	268,485	6,388	11,968	2,713	4,571	306,369
1987	28,394	474,400	12,672	14,967	7,251	8,617	546,310
1988	21,232	513,400	8,406	15,212	9,498	8,383	576,134
1989	25,185	277,232	6,868	8,453	26,461	11,840	356,040
1990	30,551	251,183	8,206	10,493	33,544	13,123	347,100
1991	73,495	228,945	13,177	21,158	37,142	15,029	390,362
1992	120,308	154,170	50,063	58,058	52,961	20,593	456,153
1993	157,836	140,702	95,106	112,884	101,380	30,649	638,557
1994	159,828	234,904	129,077	112,135	56,435	45,564	737,943
1995	352,614	202,786	165,601	142,594	40,842	74,251	978,688
1996	450,199	223,509	166,716	198,599	63,338	107,796	1,210,157
1997	549,692	237,690	200,748	155,113	56,821	116,827	1,316,891
1998	652,881	254,887	168,965	156,911	9,659	118,861	1,362,164
1999	673,263	453,110	91,791	163,352	31,617	96,527	1,509,660
2000	554,432	658,325	139,043	174,870	58,732	91,040	1,676,442
2001	459,286	695,229	119,626	122,926	45,974	58,172	1,501,213

Source: Korea Automobile Manufacturers Association, Korean Automobile Industry, 1989–2002.

Asia and the Middle East. Thus, the US experience enabled Korean automobile companies to expand very rapidly into other markets. During this period, Daewoo established overseas sales offices whereas Hyundai and Kia began their offshore Knock Down (KD) assembly in Asia, Europe and South America. The EU market became the major export destination in the first half of 1990s but by the second half of 1990s, the export destinations of Korean auto companies had become more diversified. However, after the 1997 economic crisis, exports to industrialised countries regained their former importance.

International network and global production

During the 1990s, substantial changes took place in international business. One of the important changes was the unprecedented increase in strategic alliances, both within and across the countries.[10] The international automobile industry is a very good example of how most of the major producers have established international networks within strategic alliances in many areas including: model sharing, supply of parts, marketing and technology development. Table 3.10 shows trends in global alliance networks in 1985, 1990 and 1995. Over a period of 10 years, the total number of strategic alliances (for technology transfer) across the 4 groups of companies increased more than 3 times, with the Japanese and European companies leading the trend. However, the Korean companies only began to be connected to the global networks in the early 1990s.

Table 3.10 Number of strategic alliances with foreign companies

Provider[a]	*Receiver*[b]				
	Japanese Co	*US Co*	*European Co*	*Korean Co*	*Total*
1985					
Japanese Co	4	8	1	4	17
US Co	5	0	0	2	7
European Co	1	3	14	0	18
Korean Co	0	0	0	0	0
Total	10	11	15	6	42
1990					
Japanese Co	8	19	15	4	46
US Co	10	2	3	4	19
European Co	8	2	35	1	46
Korean Co	0	1	0	0	1
Total	26	24	53	9	112
1995					
Japanese Co	16	22	18	7	63
US Co	12	2	4	4	22
European Co	10	3	34	3	50
Korean Co	2	2	0	0	4
Total	40	29	56	14	139

Source: Kim (1996: 152).

Notes

a Companies that provide finished cars, parts and technology under a strategic alliance.

b Companies that receive finished cars, parts and technology under a strategic alliance.

Although the basic production system of the Korean automobile industry was established according to the Fordist model, technical improvement in the Korean automobile industry during the period of rapid expansion was heavily influenced by the Japanese companies.[11] Table 3.11 shows the details of the technical transfers from overseas to the Korean automobile industry and indicates that technical transfers from Japan were most important, with the exception of 1993. It was not difficult for Korean firms to understand the Japanese management system, due to the geographical proximity, combined with the understanding of language and culture. As a result, many large Korean companies adopted similar strategies when they began to enter the international market. Korean firms tried to introduce some features of the Japanese management strategy as well. Both Hyundai and Kia tried to adopt a lean production system, initially developed by Toyota. However, the basic production system remained a Fordist linear system, resulting in a combination of lean production and Fordist production (Lansbury and Woo 2002). Table 3.12 summarises the major strategic alliances of the Korean automobile industry in 1995. Hyundai had technical alliances with Mitsubishi for developing the engine system, while Kia had technical alliances with Mazda for the production system.[12] Daewoo had the most diverse strategic alliances: with GM, Honda, Isuzu, Suzuki and Volvo.

Table 3.11 Technical transfer to the automobile industry from overseas

Country	*1989*	*1990*	*1991*	*1992*	*1993*
United States	11 (1,540)	6 (3,071)	8 (2,854)	14 (14,355)	12 (5,535)
Japan	37 (12,965)	28 (11,877)	27 (11,546)	40 (16,299)	42 (57,672)
United Kingdom	1 (347)	9 (23,750)	7 (5,777)	13 (23,735)	11 (16,554)
Germany	3 (2,416)	8 (5,157)	4 (79,763)	5 (632)	7 (102,801)
Others	4 (12,872)	6 (9,057)	4 (98)	7 (12,055)	13 (8,354)

Source: Kim (1995: 33).

Note
Unit: Number of project (US$1,000).

Table 3.12 Major strategic alliances of the Korean automobile industry in 1995

Company	*With industrialised country*	*With developing countries*
Hyundai	Mitsubishi: Capital (11.5%) Technology Parts	Turkey: Production of passenger cars Indonesia: Assembly of passenger cars Egypt: Assembly and production, supply of parts
Kia	Ford: Capital (10%) Mazda: Capital (8%), technology, production	Brazil: Joint venture for production Pakistan: Assembly India: Plan to have joint venture
Daewoo	GM: Production (parts) Honda: Technology (legend) Isuzu: Technology (truck, bus) Suzuki: Technology (light cars) Volvo: Technology (large truck)	Uzbekistan: Assembly of passenger cars Tashkent: Plan to build an assembly plant

Source: Kim (1995: 70).

The strategic alliances of Korean firms with the companies in DCs were mainly in terms of technical alliances, whereas those with LDCs were mainly joint-venture agreements for assembly, marketing and sales. LDCs usually provided land for production sites, information gathering and the connections to the local agents, including local governments. Most of the overseas assembly plants of the Korean automobile companies were joint ventures.

Table 3.13 shows the subsidiaries of the three Korean automobile companies which were established between 1980 and 2001. The process of globalisation of the Korean automobile industry can be broadly divided into four major stages, with a progression towards globalisation at each stage. From 1980 to 1990 was a period of export through sales agents; from 1990 to 1994 was a period of expansion through sales offices; from 1995 to 1998 was a beginning of overseas production through KD assembly; and the period from 1999 to 2001 saw the relocation of complete production system overseas.[13]

During the first period (1980–1990) the three Korean auto companies relied mainly on the direct exports through independent sales agents in host countries. Overseas subsidiaries provided the representative offices which handled information gathering, coordination with the local sales agents and public relations. During the second stage (1990–1994), many sales offices were established as subsidiaries in Europe and LDCs, while Kia commenced KD assembly in LDCs. Daewoo's efforts to globalise were most prominent and aggressive in this stage, partly to overcome the limitation of being a follower in the domestic market. During the third period (1995–1998), all three companies actively established the assembly plants in LDCs, most of them being joint ventures with local partners. The protection of the automobile industry was very strong in LDCs and there were no other ways to establish the assembly plants in these countries. Naturally, there were transfers of technical and management know-how through the joint ventures. However, as they were mainly assembly plants, based on labour-intensive technology, human resource management became the key to the successful operation of subsidiaries in LDCs.[14]

The current period has seen the complete relocation of automobile production to other countries. Although Hyundai opened its first overseas production plant in Canada in 1985 with a production capacity of 100,000 units per annum, it was closed in 1993 after prolonged operational difficulties.[15] Excluding the investment to Canada then, the fourth period begins with the opening of Hyundai's plant in India and subsequently China in 2001.[16] Kia also commenced complete production in China in 2001. Thanks to the successful establishment and operation of Hyundai Motors India (HMI), Hyundai decided to re-enter the North American market in 2002 and completed the construction of the production plant in 2004. This is a milestone in the history of the Korean automobile industry, indicating that an era of global production has begun.

Concluding remarks

In this chapter, the growth of the Korean automobile industry was analysed with particular attention to its globalisation process. Several important observations can be made. First, the growth of the Korean automobile companies shows three distinct stages of development: the import substitution period (1962–1971), 'taking off' with their own models (1972–1982) and the phase of mass production and globalisation (1983–2001). The globalisation process can be further divided into four periods: export through sales agents (1983–1990), expansion through sales offices (1990–1994), the beginning of overseas production through KD assembly (1995–1998) and the beginning of relocation of complete production systems overseas (1999–2001).

At first glance, these four stages of globalisation seem to indicate that the 'stage theory' put forward by the Scandinavian school (Johanson and Vahlne 1977) explain the Korean experiences adequately, in that the globalisation proceeded in stages. However, there are important distinctions to be made with respect to this proposition. The four-stages model assumes that the main force which enables the firm to move to the next stage is the experience accumulated during the current stage, and that globalisation would normally proceed according to the physical distance. The experiences of the Korean automobile companies are different from these expectations in two ways. First, the increase in exports took place simultaneously with the rapid expansion of the domestic sales. Due to the large-scale investments, focusing on the domestic sales would have resulted in massive excess capacities. Second, Korean firms' globalisation strategies were not carried out according to the physical distance. Subsidiaries were established in various parts of the world simultaneously, with different modes of investment in each region. Even for market-seeking investment, the market size tends to dominate the choice of location (Suh and Seo 1998, 1999; Seo and Suh 1999).

During the examination of the characteristics of the globalisation process of the Korean automobile industry, three facts were identified: (1) the growth of the Korean automobile industry depended on the expansion of international sales, (2) the Korean automobile industry began to globalise before it has developed significant competitive advantages and (3) the Korean automobile industry built its competitive advantage through its experiences in international markets.

In light of these stylised facts, most of the traditional theories of FDI have limitations in their applications to the analysis of the internationalisation of Hyundai Motors Company (HMC). First, most of the existing theories are static in nature, analysing the choice of firms at each given point in time, although some dynamic theories have been put forward recently (Teece *et al.* 1997; Teece 1998). Yet, considering the rapid changes in the competitive advantages and the internationalisation strategies of HMC, a research framework with a dynamic focus is necessary. Second, most of the existing theories regard the competitiveness of the firm as a pre-condition for internationalisation and analyse the choice of the best mode of internationalisation. As explained earlier, HMC developed and strengthened its firm-specific competitive advantage through internationalisation. Third, the dynamic theories put forward recently identify the possibility of changes in the firm's competitiveness through internalisation experiences.

In order to adequately explain the internationalisation process of the Korean automobile industry, it is necessary to use several theories jointly. In the 'taking off' period, when the Korean automobile companies first began exporting, the major sources of competitiveness were highly motivated labour, the leadership of the senior executives, including the group chairman, and support from the government. Porter's *Diamond* (1990), which tries to explain the source of competitiveness and internationalisation in terms of the home country environment, is particularly relevant.

During the first three sub-periods of mass production and globalisation (1983–1998), the bold investment made by the Korean automobile industry increased the scale of production, and became a source of competitiveness. In this period, Korean companies began accumulating firm-specific competitive

Table 3.13 Subsidiaries of Korean automobile companies

Year	*Rep. office*	*Sales*	*Research*	*KD assembly*	*Production*
1980	Japan (H[a])				
1983		Canada (H)			
1985	United States (H, 2), Canada (K[b])				Canada (H, closed in 1993)
1986			United States (H)		
1988	Japan (K)				
1989	United States (H) (Financing)		United States (K)	Philippines (K), Taiwan (K)	
1990	United Kingdom (K)	Germany (H)			
1991		Nigeria (D[c]), Algeria (D)			
1992	China (H), Germany (H),	United States (K, 2) Japan (K), Chile (D)		Venezuela (K)	
1993		Thailand (D), Columbia (D), Venezuela (D), Australia (D)		Thailand (H), Zimbabwe (H), Vietnam (K), Iran (K), Germany (K)	
1994		Austria (D), Spain (D), United Kingdom (D), Germany (D), France (D), Benelux (D), Italy (D), Hungary (D), Kazakhstan (D), Peru (D)	Japan (K), United Kingdom (D), Germany (D)	Pakistan (K), China (D)	
1995	Hong Kong (K)	Germany (K)	Germany (H)	Philippines (H) Indonesia (H) Egypt (H), India (D), Indonesia (D), China (D)	
1996	United States (H, from Canada sales)		Japan (H)	China (H), Pakistan (H) (plan), Venezuela (H), Malaysia (K), Vietnam (D), Uzbekistan (D), Iran (D), Philippines (D), Czech (D)	Romania (D), Poland (D)

1997			Turkey (H), Botswana (H)	
1998			Vietnam (H), Egypt (D)	India (H), Ukraine (D)
1999	UAE (H), Miami (H), Australia (H)		Malaysia (H), Pakistan (H), Indonesia (K), Russia (K), Brazil (K)	
2000[d]	HME	HMP (H) – Poland, HMJ (H) – Japan	Iran (H), Costa Rica (H), Indonesia (K), Turkey (K)	
2001[d]	Singapore (H)		Taiwan (H), Thailand (H)	China (H), China (K)

Source: Hyundai Motor Company, Automotive Industry, 2002.

Notes
a H: Hyundai.
b K: Kia.
c D: Daewoo.
d Projection as at 2000–2001.
HME: Hyundai Motors England.
HMP: Hyundai Motors Poland.
HMJ: Hyundai Motors Japan.

advantages. During the last sub-period of mass production and globalisation (1999–2001), the firm-specific advantages of the Korean companies began to appear. Therefore, during these periods, traditional theories of FDI, such as the Dunning's electic paradigm (1977, 1988, 1995 and 1998) and resource-based theory (Kogut and Zander 1993; Subramaniam and Venkatraman 2001) can be used to explain the internationalisation process of the Korean automobile industry, as these theories regard the accumulated firm-specific know-how as the base of the FDI.

While most of the traditional theories are silent on the process of development or accumulation of firm-specific competitive advantages, the dynamic capabilities theory put forward recently by Teece *et al.* (1997), Teece (1998) and Winter (2000) helps to explain the learning process of the Korean automobile industry through internationalisation. As these theories developed relatively recently, and should be applied to test their capacity for generalisation, more research is needed in this area.

Most of the FDI carried out by the Korean automobile companies was market oriented. Subsidiaries in DCs were mostly representative offices and sales companies. Subsidiaries in LDCs comprised sales companies and assembly plants. It is worth noting that trade-oriented investment did not exist among the subsidiaries of the Korean automobile companies. Due to the importance of the brand name, cars produced in other LDCs would find it hard to compete with domestically produced cars and those imported from DCs. With the absence of a supply chain, intra-industry trade of parts and components was not extensively developed. Technology-seeking investments were carried out by the Korean automobile industry. The establishment of R&D offices in the United States, Germany and Japan were aimed at acquiring technologies belonging to this category.

Until recently, most of the globalisation efforts by the Korean automobile industry still focused on direct export of domestic production. However, since 1997, the Korean automobile industry has re-launched its overseas production, in India, Poland, Romania and China. In 2002, Hyundai Motor Company re-entered the United States for local production. The era of global production has now begun among the Korean automobile companies.

As the Korean automobile industry has only recently begun complete production overseas, most of the parts are either produced in Korea or local countries. The extensive supply chain, and global materials management is yet to be developed for the global production system to achieve maturity. Most of the important management decisions are still made by the parent company. [17] In order to deepen the process of globalisation and maturation of the Korean automobile industry and to compete successfully in the era of global competition, the following steps must be taken. First, there must be an increase in the proportion of overseas production, as was the case with the Japanese automobile industry in the early 1990s. Second, there must be the establishment of global supply chains, both among the subsidiaries in the same region and between the parent company and its subsidiaries. Finally, global coordination of production, marketing and technology development is needed between the parent company and its subsidiaries, as well as among the subsidiaries.

4 Hyundai Motors as a global auto company

Introduction

This chapter analyses the emergence of the Hyundai Motor Company (HMC) as the major auto manufacturer in Korea and its expansion as a global producer. The chapter traces the development of HMC from its origins in the early post-war period as a vehicle repairer to the largest Korean auto manufacturer and a major global producer.

While much has been written about the emergence of American and Japanese companies as global automobile manufacturers during recent decades, relatively little attention has been paid to the Korean automobile industry which has undergone significant development since the 1980s. Despite the impact of the Asian economic crisis of the late 1990s, which saw the demise of several Korean auto companies, the HMC recovered quickly.

It is argued that much of HMC's early success depended not only on its manufacturing strategy, which enabled it to reach mass production very rapidly, but also on its employment relations strategies which, along with government policies of the time, enabled HMC to suppress trade union activity and unilaterally determine the wages and conditions of workers.

The development of the Korean automobile industry

Though the Korean automobile industry originated in the early 1930s during the period of Japanese colonial rule (1910–1945), it largely functioned as a repair shop or reproduced used cars until the early 1960s. From the early 1960s, however, the Korean automobile industry became one of the key industries in the rapid industrialisation of the Korean economy, a process initiated by a series of Five Year Economic Development Plans (FYEDP) by the Park government (1961–1979). As a part of the First and Second FYEDP (1962–1966, 1967–1971), the state encouraged the development of automobile factories for small passenger and commercial cars, such as buses and trucks. This was done by unifying various automobile companies into one for each product. This strategy enabled the industry to grow from the 'knock-down' (KD) assembly factory to self-sufficiency in manufacturing under the Localisation Plan for Imported Auto Parts from 1962 to 1967.

As a result of this policy, the Saenara Motor Company (SMC) was established and produced 1,710 and 1,063 small passenger cars in 1962 and 1963 respectively, by assembling 'semi-knock-down' (SKD) parts of the Nissan Bluebird model. These SKD parts were imported as a part of foreign capital loan and technology cooperation with the Japanese government and the Nissan Motor Company. This plan failed, however, because of a lack of foreign capital to sustain the industry and enable it to continue importing KD parts. Moreover, automobile production technologies never developed beyond basic manual production because foreign car makers were reluctant to transplant any advanced automobile production technologies to Korea, viewing the country as solely a market for export rather than local production. Thus, SMC produced only 216 cars in 1964 and 106 in 1965. Eventually, the company was taken over by Shinjin Motors (the former name of the Daewoo Motor Company (DMC)) in 1965. The government plan for the localisation of auto parts only reached around 20–27 per cent during the first half of the 1960s (Oh, Woncheol 1996; Kim, Wangun 1993: 27).

Despite the failure of this initial venture into automobile manufacturing, the Korean government's initiatives resulted in a change in the Korean automobile industry towards KD assembly production under business partnership arrangements with international car makers. Asia Motors negotiated a partnership with Fiat Co. of Italy in 1965, while the HMC and the Ford Motor Company became partners in 1967. These partnerships led to the production of Fiat and Ford models using imported complete knock down (CKD) parts under capital and production technology agreements. Shinjin Motors took over the Saenara Motor Company in 1965 and produced Toyota models with the support of the Toyota Motor Company. As a result, the production capacity of the Korean automobile industry increased from 4,000 passenger cars in 1965, to 15,000 in 1968 and to 28,000 by 1971 (Automobile Manufacturing Association of Korea 1983: 689).

On the basis of its success in building up national infrastructure and in developing light industries by way of rapid industrialisation, under the First and Second FYEDP, the Park government undertook to develop heavy chemical and machinery industries under the Third and Fourth FYEDPs (1972–1976, 1977–1981). The automobile industry became one of the strategic targets of these economic plans, with shipbuilding and chemical industries particularly targeted because of their flow-on effects on the development of related machinery industries. Therefore, the government directly guided the expansion of the automobile industry by launching the *Long-term Plan for Development of the Automobile Industry* in 1973. This Plan set out to lead to the production of a Korean low-cost model as a long-term export product under the KD assembly production system. To achieve this goal, the government required the automobile industry to standardise and localise auto parts and to establish a mass production system. This state-guided policy resulted in restructuring among automobile makers: Asia Motor Company was taken over by Kia in 1976 as Asia had failed to satisfy the guidelines set out by the state. Shinjin, in turn, was taken over by the Daewoo Motor Company in 1978 as its business partner, General Motors, refused to develop a Korean-sourced model and the firm went into bankruptcy. After the breakdown of its partnership with Ford in 1973, HMC was successful in developing its own model, the *Pony*, with the assistance of production technology and capital from Mitsubishi. From this period, these three major motor companies were central to the development of the Korean automobile industry until the late 1990s. During this period, the production capacity of Korean car makers dramatically increased from 63,100 units in 1973 to 280,000 units by 1979, including buses and trucks (Korean Industrial Bank 1984: 355).

The Hyundai Motor Company: origins and development

Hyundai Business Group set up its first business in 1946 with an automobile repair shop. This small business was converted into a construction business in 1947 by the foundation of the Hyundai Engineering and Construction Co. (HECC). During the Korean War (1950–1953) and the First and Second FYEDP (1962–1971) period, HECC established a monopoly position in the construction industry in Korea. A variety of factors aided Hyundai's entry into the automobile industry.

First, it was the personal ambition of Hyundai's founder, Chung Juyung, who was exposed to the automobile business in the late 1930s and 1940s while operating a repair shop. Second, under the state-guided economy, Hyundai was able to benefit from the government economic policies that promoted heavy chemical and machinery industries. This was the crucial factor that enabled Hyundai to diversify away from its concentration in the construction industry and enabled it to expand into new and large-scale industries such as shipbuilding and the automobile industry. Hyundai also obtained low-interest loans from the state-controlled banking system. Last, but most importantly, these new industries enabled Hyundai to expand its size and diversify into related businesses and to maximise economies of scale and scope. These new industries, in turn, enhanced the competitiveness of Hyundai's construction business by mechanising the organisation of construction work with the production of heavy construction equipment and steel structures. Thus, the Hyundai Motor Company was established in 1968 while Hyundai Heavy Industries began in 1974 to facilitate its expansion into the shipbuilding and heavy machinery industries.

In a manner analogous to other Korean automobile companies, HMC began as a CKD assembler under an Assembly and Technological Cooperation Agreement with the Ford Motor Company. In early 1973, the partnership between HMC and Ford ended because of disagreements over managerial control of HMC and the international market strategy of Ford which sought to confine HMC to its domestic market, under the managerial authority of Ford, with respect to key business decisions. Moreover, the government demanded that automobile companies develop their own model utilising CKD assembly and restricted foreign car imports and, later, even CKD products. In this context, HMC had a considerable competitive incentive to develop its own model.

As a result, in 1976, HMC produced its first original model, the *Pony* (with over 90 per cent of parts sourced locally), using a low-cost approach (around US$2,000) for the assembly of a small-sized passenger car (under 1,500cc) with the technological support and 10 per cent capital participation of Mitsubishi Motors of Japan. The successful development of this model resulted in Hyundai becoming the top car maker in Korea as its market share rose sharply from 19 per cent in 1970, to 39 per cent in 1973 and to 58 per cent in 1977 (HECC 1982: 52). Based on the success of the *Pony*, an initial mass production system was established to produce 100,000 passenger cars annually in 1979, assisted by the development of its second model, *Pony II*. As a result, HMC's sales increased sharply from 528 million won in 1968 to 26,092 million won in 1974 to 224,957 million won in 1980 (*Monthly Chungkyeong Munhwa* February 1986: 166–167; HMC 1987: 34–38; HMC 1992: 362–364, 1084).

With the rapid expansion of its mass production capacity, HMC developed a variety of models ranging from the *Excel* (1,400cc, 1985), *Stellar* (1,439cc and 1,597cc, 1982), *Sonata* (1,800cc and 2,000cc, 1985) and *Elantra* (1,500cc and 1,800cc, 1990) through cooperation with Mitsubishi. Canada was HMC's first overseas market and opened a plant there in 1983. With the *Pony*, HMC sold 79,072 cars, or 7 per cent of the Canadian small passenger car market, in 1985. This success enabled HMC to make a significant market entry into the United States in 1986 with its competitively-priced *Excel*. This model sold 168,882 cars, the third largest number of sales in the small-sized and imported passenger category in the United States in 1986 and again in 1987. HMC also enjoyed rapid growth during the 1980s and its domestic market and its share of passenger cars was consistently in excess of 70 per cent during the first half of the 1980s. Overall, HMC's total sales grew from 5,774 hundred million won in 1983 to 28,402 hundred million won in 1987 (HMC 1992: 518–596, 1081–1110).

From the late 1980s, however, HMC suffered a serious structural crisis similar to other Korean automobile companies, due to various factors. First, from the late 1980s the Korean economy had been under considerable international pressure to remove government protection of its industries and to open its market to increased foreign competition. This policy had a particularly serious impact on the Korean automobile industry, the main target of international pressure. Moreover, Korean car makers faced increased market protection in export markets. Furthermore, HMC's monopoly in the domestic market for small-sized cars was broken by Daewoo, Kia and Asia Motors in the aftermath of the ending of the government's monopoly policy in 1986. Ssangyong and Samsung also entered this fiercely competitive market in 1988 and 1994, respectively.

Second, the international automobile industry underwent major restructuring resulting from over-supply, excessive production capacity and intensive competition from the 1980s. This was triggered by the big three US car makers, Ford, GM and Chrysler, once they recovered from their structural problems in the early 1980s. The restructuring of the international automobile industry gave rise to a number of strategic alliances between international car majors via merger and acquisitions or business partnerships. This was initiated to achieve economies of scale and production and to increase the companies' respective positions in the international automobile market. This trend in the international automobile industry forced HMC to ensure its survival in the international market via strategic alliances with other car makers or, alternatively, to expand by itself.

Third, changes in the socio-political environment in the direction of a more democratic society forced the Korean *chaebol*, or family-controlled large conglomerates, such as Hyundai, to fragment in the face of strident public criticism of their corrupt relationship with previous governments and dominance over the Korean economy[1].

This resulted in the break-up of the Hyundai Business Group into a number of smaller conglomerates such as the HMC automobile group and HECC construction group.[2] This implied that HMC might no longer benefit from large economies of scale and scope resulting from the vertical and horizontal integration of various Hyundai businesses.[3]

Fourth, since the late 1980s, Korean society has been under transition from the authoritarian political society to more democratic ethos, as a result of nation-wide democratic movement in the late 1980s. Within Hyundai this resulted in the emergence of a militant trade union movement in Korea. Hyundai trade unions have played a central role in the growth of a national independent trade union movement in Korea. The growing industrial militancy of the HMC union significantly undermined HMC's traditional low-cost strategy.

Taken together, these factors explain HMC's loss of competitiveness in both domestic and international markets. Its domestic market share declined from 76 per cent in 1986 to 56 per cent in 1989 and to 42 per cent in 1993. Its exports overseas similarly decreased from 426,000 passenger cars in 1987 to 256,000 cars in 1991 (HMC 1992: 1081–1110; 1999: 16). In 1993, in response to such difficulties, HMC outlined a long-term business strategy, the so-called 'Global Top-10', whereby it aimed to be one of the world's ten largest car makers by 2000, compared with twentieth position in 1992.

To achieve this goal, HMC aggressively expanded its production capacity in order to match that of other top ten global car makers. This expansion was coupled with HMC's globalisation strategy. To enhance its cost competition and expand into new markets, HMC aggressively globalised its production systems, particularly in developing countries such as Turkey, India, China and Malaysia. HMC also established new automobile plants in Korea with annual production of 300,000 units. HMC extended its passenger cars from the small-medium sized to the large class, such as the 4,000cc model, and developed various models such as a sport style passenger car, with the improvement of production technologies. HMC also moved away from its dependence on the US market and sought to increase exports to other countries[4]. As a result, its exporting market diversified from 65 countries in 1986 to 141 in 1994 (HMC 1992: 628–754; HMC 1994).

In the course of implementing its Global Top-10 strategy, HMC was severely affected by the Asian economic crisis in late 1997 when the Korean banking system was unable to repay its large external debt and could not maintain the stability of the currency. In the fallout from the crisis, the Korean won sharply depreciated from 844.20 won to US$1 in 1996 to 14,15.20 won to US$1 in 1997. This foreign exchange crisis directly undermined the financial capacity of debt-based growth of the large Korean conglomerates. Kia Motors was already bankrupt from 1996 as it was unable to sustain its heavy debts. Daewoo Motor Company also became bankrupt and was in the process of being merged with or acquired by either a domestic or international car maker by the late 1990s. HMC was also severely affected and its rate of production declined to a mere 40 per cent of production capacity. HMC responded to the crisis by cutting its production costs and reducing Foreign Direct Investment (FDI).

At the same time, the crisis provided an opportunity for HMC to expand its business size in the automobile industry. HMC took over Kia Motors in 1998 and restored its dominant market position of over 70 per cent of the domestic market in 1999, while increasing its production capacity to over 2 million units in passenger cars. As a result, HMC succeeded in becoming the world's tenth largest car manufacturer in terms of production capacity in 1999 (*Chosun Iibo* 28 Apr. 2000). The takeover of Kia Motors by HMC was also motivated by a desire to protect its domestic market position from international competitors entering into Korean car market by taking over other ailing car makers. By the late 1990s, HMC had gradually recovered from the economic crisis and recommenced its policy of globalising its production systems. For example, HMC finished the construction of plants in China in 1999 and began the construction of plants in Indonesia and Brazil in 2000. All together, HMC planned to produce over 1 million units from these overseas plants in the future. Table 4.1 provides details of HMC's overseas plants. Table 4.2 shows changes in actual outcomes of production, including the overseas production bases. It shows that although HMC's production capacity increased, its actual production levels had declined, as a result of the economic crisis.

Table 4.1 Overseas plants of HMC, 2000

Country	*Turkey*	*India*	*China*	*Malaysia*	*Total*
Amount invested	124	393	36	54	607
Capital	80	212	28	30.4	350.4
Production capacity	90,000	120,000	60,000	60,000	330,000
Business partner	HMC: 50% Kibar: 50%	HMC: 100%	HMC: 21% China: 50% YS: 29%	HMC: 15% Malay: 70% Renault: 15%	

Source: Derived from various HMC internal documents, 2000.

Notes
Production capacity is based on three shifts of production.
Unit: million US$.

Table 4.2 Changes in the production outcomes by production sites, 1996–1998

Year	*Domestic plants*	*Overseas plants*	*Total*
1996	1,341,990	15,980	1,357,970
1997	1,310,358	36,606	1,346,964
1998	845,496	52,500	897,996

Source: Derived from HMC (1999: 73).

Note
The production outcome of overseas plants includes CKD parts that exported to overseas partners.

The changing nature of production systems within HMC

The complete knocked down (CKD) assembly stage: 1968–1973

The first automobile production system in HMC was set up in 1968 through the Overseas Assembler and Technological Assistance Agreement (1968) between HMC and Ford. This production system was designed to assemble a CKD model for a small passenger car, the *Cortina*, and a *D-series*, both Ford models. The 'Fordist' assembly line became the model for HMC's production system in the 1960s and HMC used Ford's machines and equipment. About 50 HMC engineers were trained overseas by Ford to install and operate assembly lines under the technological supervision of Ford's engineers. Its production system was organised into five basic lines: body welding, metal, painting, trimming and chassis lines.[5] A knocked down (KD) material supply system, known as the Unitisation Trolley System, was designed along Fordist lines to supply small boxes of the necessary KD materials for one car to each assembly line. The first CKD-assembled passenger car, the *Cortina*, was produced in 400 minutes, along 5 sequential production lines each of 80 minutes duration, and involved 349 production workers (HMC 1987: 38–70, 110; HMC 1992: 1085).

The production processes of HMC were limited to those which had been developed for mass production on the basis of mechanisation. These limitations were the result of the dependency of HMC on manual jobs because of a shortage of supportive machinery and equipment and a lack of management skills. For example, until the mid-1970s, a manual chain conveyor system was mainly used on the moving assembly lines for KD materials (Kim, Hyeoungki 1988: 239), and the Unitisation Trolley System was also operated manually; only a minimal amount of advanced machinery and equipment was installed on each line.[6] Further, the assembly lines were not configured according to product, so that cars and buses or truck lines were mixed (HMC 1987: 63–64, 102). Although various quality-management techniques and production plans were transferred from Ford to HMC through management training programmes, these techniques had a limited application in HMC until the mid-1970s because of a lack of understanding and management skills during this period (HMC 1987: 47–69).

Owing to the limitations of its production system, HMC management sought to develop more rational production practices, but practical change was limited. Skilled workers were recruited from mechanical repair shops, factories and arsenals and assigned to the production lines indiscriminately. Foremen were put in charge of sections with formal regulations. The production lines were operated mainly by semi-skilled workers fulfilling a range of tasks, having been trained at HMC's Vocational Training Centre (HMC 1987: 103). Assembly line workers put in two shifts a day while senior management would often directly guide operations. Professional engineers trained on Ford's production systems acted as informal foremen under the supervision of Ford's despatched engineers. However, both engineers and skilled workers were limited in their control over production process because of senior management's involvement in every detail of the assembly line (HMC 1987: 52–96).

Towards mass production systems at HMC: 1974–1982

Following the development of its own model small passenger car, the *Pony*, in 1974, HMC began to develop mass production systems and convert its production process from manual and small-scale assembly to mechanised large-scale assembly. HMC's production capacity expanded from 50,000 vehicles in 1974, to 100,000 in 1979 and to 300,000 in 1982 (HMC 1992: 362–550, 1111). As shown in Figure 4.1, the five main lines of assembly in the CKD stage were transformed into eight workshops for passenger cars. In addition to engine and transmission, forging and foundry shops, there were 31 assembly lines. This basic work process

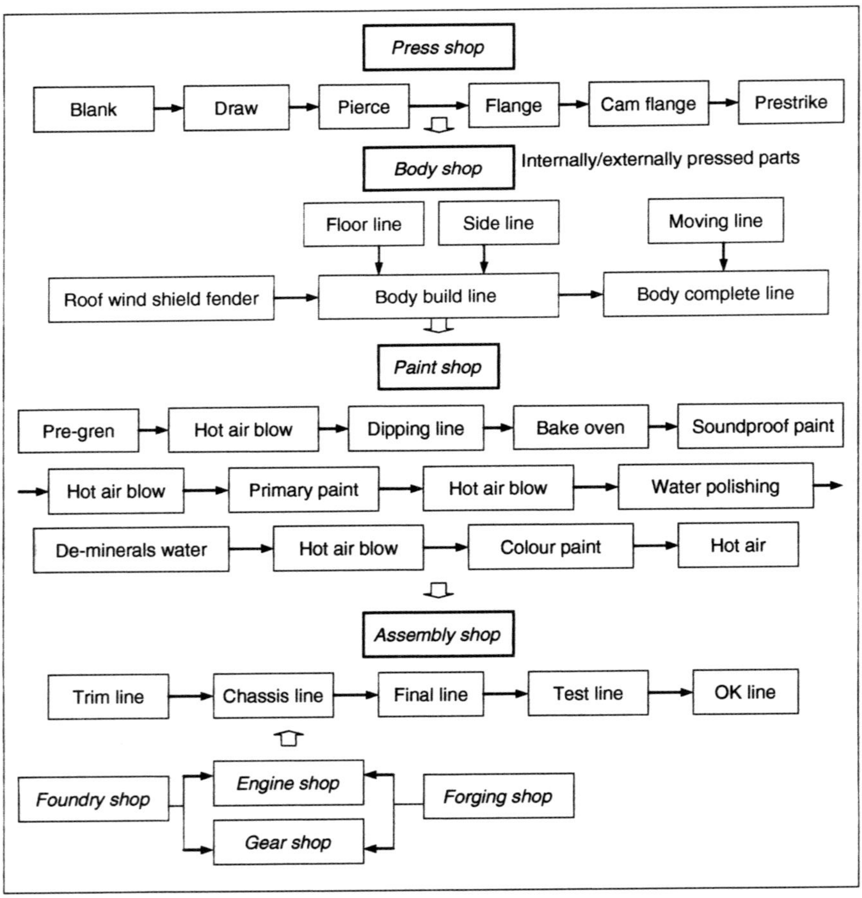

Figure 4.1 Production structure of HMC for passenger cars, 1975.

Source: Derived from HECC (1982: 1637–1641); HMC (1992: 395–397).

in the initial stage of mass production was further modified, in 1979, with the expansion of HMC's production capacity to 100,000 cars a year. Following its success in the domestic market with the *Pony*, HMC developed a new model, the *Excel*, for the international market in 1982, and the production capacity was expanded to 300,000 a year (HMC 1992: 423–518).

Fordist production methods largely determined HMC's approach to the production process, although Japanese production systems were used in the management of work relations practices. The Fordist structure was applied to the mass production system mainly because of Ford's initial influence which had instilled a Ford production mentality among HMC management. Furthermore, at this time, the Fordist production system was the most influential method of assembly for developing countries like Korea, where few alternatives existed. Mechanisation and mass production were sustained by the standardisation of auto parts through HMC's subcontractors who, until 1975, produced 90 per cent of the company's total auto parts. Nationally, the *Korean Standardisation of Quality Regulations* encouraged the standardisation of parts to promote mass production in the automobile industry, thereby achieving significant economies of scale (Korean Automobile Manufacturers Association 1987; HMC 1992: 364–544).

Computer Aided Design and Manufacturing were also intensively developed, particularly after 1979, further promoting the 'scientific' management of mass production at HMC through pre-planning and minimising material waste. Part supply was computerised by the Assembly Line Control system thereby reducing design man hours by 35 per cent in 1979: the 1,000 hours per month expended on remedying production faults in 1982 was reduced to below 100 hours in 1983, and hourly production capacity was increased from 13 vehicles in 1978 to 30 in 1979 (Lee, Jongseon 1989: 28–30; HMC 1992: 452–537).

HMC management's approach to the work organisation and practices was influenced by foreign companies and engineers. For example, in 1974, foreign technicians were employed to meet a skill gap and all aspects of production were under their supervision.[7] However, the most influential company was the Mitsubishi Motor Company because of its direct business partnership with HMC. The Mitsubishi Motor Company was not only a technological supporter, but was actively involved in the design of the first full automobile manufacturing systems of HMC through the technological and managerial training of HMC's employees and the supply of production equipment and machines in 1974.[8] Finally, in the course of the development of a mass production system, to achieve an annual capacity of 300,000 cars in 1982, Mitsubishi made a strategic investment in HMC equal to 10 per cent of HMC's total capitalisation. HMC and Mitsubishi also entered into an Enhanced Technological Cooperation Agreement to supply various auto parts such as transaxles, chassis components and engines (HMC 1992: 372–518).

As a result, elements of the Japanese style of labour management were transferred from Mitsubishi to HMC to better regulate and enhance production. In order to increase productivity and reduce production costs, HMC introduced Japanese-style quality management techniques, including a quality control system (1975), a job suggestion system (1975) and an occupational invention system (1976) with financial rewards (1976)[9]. Quality control activities were further promoted through the government policies with its *National Competition in Quality Management and Standardisation Campaign* (1975), *Gojang Semaulundong* (*New Factory Campaign,* 1975) and *Quality Management Control Activities* (1976). In 1979, HMC expanded its fledgling Organisation of Quality Control Section to become the Total Quality Control Division with 670 quality units. Under the Division's leadership, initiatives, such as the *Hyundai Individual Worker Suggestion Campaign*, the *Elimination Campaign for Irrational, Unbalanced, Unnecessary Actions in Production Lines* and the *Internal Standardisation Movement*, were introduced to encourage participation for production cost savings and quality improvement. As a result of these quality control activities and suggestion systems, HMC saved production costs of 1.4 billion won by 1979 and 4 billion won by 1982 (HMC 1992: 391–507; Interview with HMC TQC specialist 24 August 1994)

HMC introduced various regulations to institutionalise all production activities to assist management, including *Quality Control Management Regulations* (1976), *Transfer and Employment Regulations for Technical Workers* (1976), *Employees' Move Regulations* (1978), *Production Management Regulations* (1979) and *Work Process Inspection Regulations* (1979) (HMC 1992: 465, 506–507). All these developments in production practices brought about changes in the organisation of production processes of HMC, resulting in the professional engineer becoming central to their operation. This allowed senior management to devote more time to senior level managerial activities and skilled workers were more efficiently utilised (HMC 1992: 465, 506–507).

The changes in the organisation of production at HMC between the 1960s and 1970s are shown in Figure 4.2. Yet, in spite of these developments, production at HMC remained rather elementary when compared with that of today. For example, foremen did not have job security under the formal employment system, and their authority remained ill-defined until the early 1980s (Bae, Kyuhan 1983: 82–84; Kang, Sudol 1987: 38–83; HMC 1992: 387–388, 408).

Mass production system and its changes: from the 1980s to the early 1990s

Following the successful launch of its initial mass production system for domestic and overseas markets in the early 1980s, the production capacity of HMC expanded rapidly from 110,000 units in 1983 to 300,000 units in 1985 and to 720,000 units in 1988. A second factory boosted HMC's annual car production by 300,000. In 1990, a third factory was completed with the projected capacity of another 240,000 passenger cars a year. By 1990, HMC's annual production capacity exceeded 1 million vehicles, including trucks and buses. At the same time, HMC developed a variety of passenger car models, from small to medium sized, with the technological assistance of the Mitsubishi Motor Company[10] (HMC 1992: 518–519, 551–688; *Chosun Ilbo* 7 December 1994; Kong, Jaewuk 1994: 46–47) (see Table 4.3).

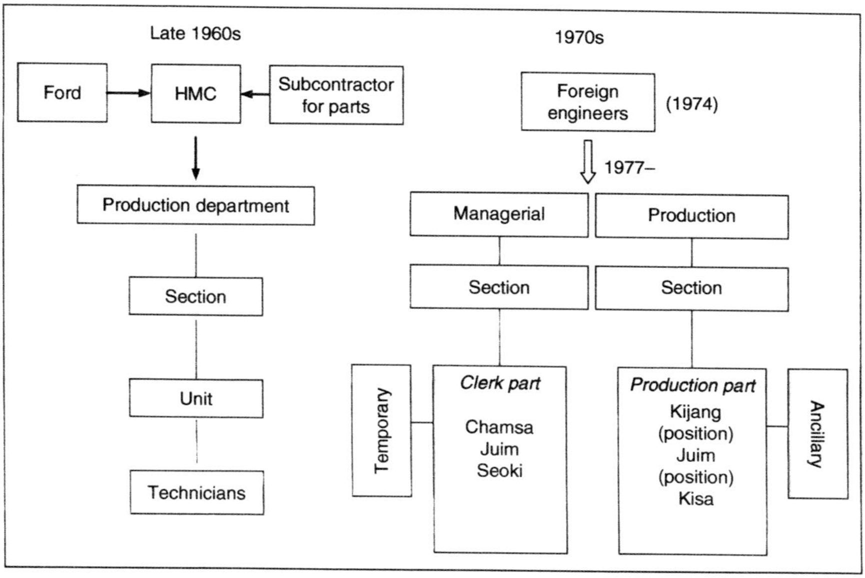

Figure 4.2 Organisational structure of production work practices of HMC, 1960s and 1970s.

Source: HMC (1987: 34–69; 1992: 463–464).

Note

In 1977, the Kisa position was introduced in the production line to enhance workplace skills and experiences.

Table 4.3 Production capacity of HMC at Ulsan plant, since 1990

Type	*First factory*	*Second factory*	*Third factory*	*Fourth factory*	*Fifth factory*	*Total*
Passenger	350,000	300,000	240,000			890,000
Truck				118,000		118,000
Bus					4,000	4,000
Total						1,012,000

Source: HMC (1992: 688).

HMC's production systems have changed in response to new market demands as well as the emergence of a mass trade union movement which sought to increase worker influence. Production has intensified since the mid-1980s through automation and mechanisation. HMC has sought to increase productivity and minimise the involvement of the unions. HMC invested considerable effort in improving its production management in order to better integrate work processes into increasingly mechanised, technologically sophisticated mass production systems. Computerisation, for example, made it possible to develop the centralised control of production, including that of subcontractors.

Table 4.4 shows the sequence and extent of the technological upgrading of HMC's production lines. Upgrading began in its first factory connected with the release of the *Excel* in 1985. Since then, HMC's production technology has become increasingly automated. As shown in Figure 4.3, this trend is apparent in the production systems of HMC's third factory constructed in 1990 for the *Elantra* and designed to produce simultaneously various numbers of similar models.

Table 4.4 Changes in major production machinery and equipment for passenger car production in HMC, 1985–1994

Shop	*1985* *First factory* *Small sized passenger car* Excel	*1990–1994* *Third factory* *Small/medium sized passenger car* Elantra
Capacity	Annually 300,000 cars constructed 1985	Annually 240,000 cars constructed 1990
Mold	Full control of molding production by CAD/CAM system	Full control of molding production by CAD/CAM system Simulation techniques
Press	Various Press cushion sets Bolsters for blanking press High efficiency of Transfer Presses (producing 270 sheets)	94% of automation by establishment of Tendom Presses lines
Paint	Electronic deposit equipment Auto spray system to semi-full dipping method Anion to cation method	87 Micro Bell automatic painters 18 industrial robots Full dipping method High Build Cation
Body	Various Multi-welding equipment for 390 spot welding Drop lifters Power & free overhead conveyor 6 angles of multi-joint sports Shuttle system Manual fitting moving parts Various welding industrial robots 1 Air press for plate metal press Automatic part supply under computer system	97% of overall automation by introduction of 267 industrial robots 100% of Floor Complete Line Automatic Fitting Jigs Various semi-divided air presses Floor Respot process for multiple works
Assembly	Tire sub assembly machining centre Automatic fuel inserters Shuttle lines Automatic supply of part under computer system	Two divided shuttle lines for automation Introduced Doorless line

Sources: Derived from HMC (1992: 568–730); Park, Joonshik (1991: 109–120); Lee, Jongseon (1989: 28–30); Kim, Hyeoungki (1988: 239–240); HECC (1982: 1638–1641); Lee, Younghee (1994: 150); Roh, Honghyeong (1992: 41–52).

Table 4.5 Changes in the number of industrial robots by type of usage, HMC, 1984–1990

Type	*1984*	*1985*	*1986*	*Total 1984–1986*	*1987*	*1988*	*1989*	*1990*	*Total (Ratio%) 1984–1990*
Spot welding	6	11	9	26	190	26	243	198	683(71.7)
Arc welding	18	4	13	35	55	8	21	19	138(14.5)
Sealing		3	2	5	10	5	25	26	71(7.4)
Painting					2		4	22	28(2.9)
Handling			2	2	1		2	11	16(1.7)
Etc.							3	13	16(1.7)
Total	24	18	26	68	258	39	298	289	952(100.0)

The introduction of industrial robots in the mid-1980s enabled the mechanisation of HMC's production lines to be combined with automation. The number of industrial robots sharply increased from 68 in 1984 to 884 between 1984 and 1990. Skilled tasks such as welding, where 85 per cent of total industrial robots were assigned, were the main targets for automation. Automation accelerated in the 1990s with 1,355 industrial robots being installed on various parts of the production lines between 1991 and 1995. As a result, the earlier single-model mass production system was transformed to allow various models to be produced concurrently. In the second factory, for example, various medium-sized passenger cars, such as the *Sonata* and the *Grandeur* were produced simultaneously (HMC 1992: 568–730; Roh, Honghyeong 1992: 53) (see Table 4.5).

The training practices of HMC were also modified to incorporate developments arising from automation. Compared with the basic training courses for semi-skilled workers in the 1970s, various training institutes such as welding school (1986), assembly school (1991) and automation school (1991) were established to enhance the skills of production workers so that they could better support the professional engineers. In 1986, 22,879 trainees undertook an average of 54.6 hours of training; in 1991, this had risen to 99,994 trainees and an average of 74.4 hours training (HMC Production Technology Department 1992; Kim, Wangun 1993: 280–281; Lee, Younghee 1994: 165–168). Quality management techniques also improved production operations. The number of quality control units increased from 670 in 1979 to 1,700 in 1987. In 1990, quality management activities were transferred to business divisions for a more context-sensitive application (HMC 1992: 728–729).

The changing nature of employment relations at HMC

Initial developments in employment relations at HMC: 1968–1974

The historical development of personnel management policies and practices at HMC owed much to developments within HECC and the Hyundai Business Group. This was because of the role of the HECC in the growth of the Hyundai

Business Group. HECC functioned as a mother company for other associated companies founded later, such as HMC and HHI. In 1968, an automobile task force team was set up as a department of HECC and became a central element of the management hierarchy of HMC. Thus, basic employment policies and practices transferred to HMC were compatible with those of HECC. For example, the *Rules of Employment* and personnel assessment system of HECC was applied to HMC, modified to suit its particular circumstances. HMC was one of the core subsidiary companies of the Hyundai Business Group, so business and management policies were under the central control of Hyundai top management. The employment relations policies of HMC were also monitored by Hyundai top management.

From its inception, HMC introduced a range of employment codes to formalise its control over workforce such as the *Rules of Employment, Personnel Code, Wage Code* (2. 1968), *Organisational Structure Code* (8. 1968) and *Rules of Night Shift* (10. 1968). The employment and production regulations introduced in 1968 are shown in Table 4.6. Managerial employees, including professional engineers, were organised into seven classes and production workers were divided into two classes. Minimum service years for promotion to the next class were provided. Fixed wage policies were structured alongside the employment structure, especially for the managerial group. With basic standard wages in each class, the fixed amount of annual wage increment was determined in line with the grade of employment, with a different amount payable for each employment class. For example, employees in the first class were given a 2,000 won annual increment while those in the fifth class received between 1,200 and 1,000 won.

Despite implementing a range of formal personnel management practices, these practices remained largely informal and *ad hoc* until the early 1970s. Furthermore, as shown in Table 4.5, production workers were organised into

Table 4.6 Employment and promotion structure of HMC, 1968

Class	*Title*		*Minimum service years for promotion*	*Qualification*
	Managerial group	*Production group*		
1	A: Bujang			⇧
	B: Chajang			
2	Kwajang		2	
3	A: Daree			
	B: Gaejang		2	University graduate
4	Sawon		3	High school graduate
5	Associate-sawon	General		
6	Driver, telephone operator	Daily labour		
7	Security guard, cleaner			⇩

Source: HMC (1992); Interview with a personnel specialist (10 Feb. 2000).

two classes, permanent workers and day labourers. This implied that there was no formal hierarchy in the production organisation and they were supervised directly by professional engineers.

HMC's recruitment policy at this time was largely *ad hoc*. Employees were recruited from various sources to meet HMC's increasing requirements for labour, without consideration of its business strategy. For example, about 100 workers were recruited in every month between 1968 and 1969 and the number of workers reached 2,792 in December 1969. This rapid growth of the workforce, however, resulted in a serious redundancy problem when HMC faced business recession in the early 1970s, when over 1,000 employees were made redundant. This resulted in a rapid reduction of HMC's workforce from 2,729 workers in 1969 to 1,696 in 1971.

HMC's personnel management practices comprised two basic characteristics. First, the internal labour market was divided between managerial and production employee groups. HMC management applied different employment policies to each employee group. This resulted in a clear demarcation in the internal labour market. Second, a seniority concept in employment policies and practices was developed to enhance the hierarchical structure of the internal labour market and reduce short-term labour turnover. Hence, years of service was an important criterion for wage increments and a minimum requirement for promotion.

The development of dual internal labour market under the mass production system from the 1970s to mid-1980s

From the mid-1970s, HMC established an internal labour market and formalised its *ad hoc* approach to employment relations in order to control its large-scale workforce during the introduction of mass production system in automobile manufacturing. Three major factors influenced this formalisation. First, HMC's rapid expansion of production capacity to 30,000 annual units in 1976 and 100,000 annual units in 1979 meant that employee numbers increased from 1,689 in 1973 to 3,720 in 1976 and to 12,065 in 1979. Second, in order to enhance its competitiveness, HMC was urged to manage 'scientifically' its large-scale workforce and to rationalise its labour and production costs. Third, as HMC moved from a CKD assembler to a self-standing manufacturer, it needed to urgently establish a high level of production engineering and labour-management capabilities through the development of a stable internal labour market for professional managerial and engineering employees.

In order to change its *ad hoc* approaches to labour management, extensive formalisation of employment practices were undertaken through the introduction of a range of regulations and rules. From the mid-1970s, recruitment and selection practices of HMC were extensively formalised in line with HECC's open recruitment system (ORS). This process outlined a method for recruiting university graduates who were allocated to the bottom grade of the professional management hierarchy. However, as HMC continued to suffer a shortage of professional managerial and engineering employees, the ORS was only used in a limited manner to meet situational demands. HMC continued to recruit experienced and skilled employees through informal personnel practices such as head hunting until the mid-1970s.

From the mid-1970s, the ORS was widely used as a main entry port to the HMC internal labour market. This was supported by strategic control of the Hyundai Business Group. In the 1970s, Hyundai diversified into heavy and machinery industries and in order to gain effective control over these areas of business, Hyundai established the Group Planning Office (GPO) in 1978.[11] The GPO was responsible for collectively recruiting university graduates for each subsidiary company of Hyundai. Once a year, each subsidiary of Hyundai estimated additional workforce in accordance with their circumstances. These estimates were collected by the GPO and included in the recruitment process. The period of recruitment was regularised, usually in June and/or November, to coincide with university graduation and the retirement of military officers, especially from the Reserve Officers' Training Corps.

While recruitment to management was under the central control of the GPO, production workers were recruited by the personnel departments of individual subsidiaries. From the mid-1970s, a company-level ORS began to be used as a means of recruiting production workers in HMC, although its application was somewhat limited. Recruitment of production workers remained largely dependent on informal and *ad hoc* practices, such as the personal recommendation of employees. This was largely due to the rapid expansion of HMC's production system which required a large increase in the workforce in a short period of time. Furthermore, a lack of production management capabilities and a turbulent product market limited HMC management's ability to efficiently control the size of its production workforce. Therefore, rather than regularising the recruiting period and workforce size, as in the case of the management group, HMC recruited workers by situational demands. Hence, HMC recruited 3,600 production workers in 1979 in connection with the establishment of its mass production system for 100,000 units a year. This became a serious managerial burden in 1980 when South Korea suffered the onset of an economic recession by the second oil price rise. As a result, many production workers were dismissed and the number of employees declined to 734 in 1980, and to 388 by 1982.

From the late 1970s, in response to the problems associated with a massive increase in employment, HMC management developed more formalised and methodical recruitment practices for hiring production workers, extending the application of the collective ORS to those who had not graduated from university. The previous practice of using personal recommendations for recruitment was formally recognised, upgraded and exploited as an important recruitment source of production workers. One interesting recruitment practice was using the government-subsidised vocational training centre of HMC. Candidates undertook primary technical courses in the centre in relation to automobile production processes. Once the candidates were qualified they were able to be selected. HMC was thus able to reduce managerial costs and potential risks in directly recruiting a permanent production workforce. During the 1970s, an average of 60 per cent of total regular trainees in HMC's vocational centre were employed on successful completion of their basic training courses. As a result, in 1977, HMC introduced *Employment Regulations for Trainees*, treating them as full-time workers, and more effectively integrating them into the workforce (HMC 1987: 103–105).

The promotion policies of HMC were developed to promote a seniority-based and bureaucratically structured internal labour market. After the late 1970s, mostly between January and February in each year, the recruitment and promotion systems were put into operation in conjunction with changes in top management positions at the Hyundai Business Group level.

Formal educational qualifications principally distinguished managerial, engineering and production employees. Therefore, in spite of automatic promotion after the requisite service period, production workers were limited by an educational barrier from entering the engineering and managerial group. As only a small number of higher level positions were available to production workers, promotion was much more competitive than in the professional management classes. Furthermore, because of the focus on seniority in employment practices, production workers generally had to wait until someone vacated a position. Overall, the employment practices which governed production workers were highly formalised as well as rigorously and inflexibly applied, resulting in slow and limited promotion.

Given that there were no trade unions in HMC until 1987, wages were unilaterally determined by management. From the mid-1970s, however, wage practices of HMC were increasingly formalised and a range of wage schemes were developed to support a seniority-based labour market. On the whole, professional management group was paid a monthly wage that comprised a basic wage plus various allowances such as position and seniority allowance. Annual increases were based on the consumer price index, and comparison with rival companies, as well as HMC's business profits and productivity.

Table 4.7 shows the basic hourly wage calculation according to work shift. This wage system ensured that working regular hours generated an income sufficient only for basic needs. The basic hourly wage was initially designed to promote

Table 4.7 Hourly wage calculation by work shifts in HMC used in 1983

Work shift	*Ordinary day*	*Unpaid holiday*	*Sunday and paid holiday*
Day-time shift			
08:00–17:00	1 × BHW	1.5 × BHW	2.5 × BHW
18:00–22:00	1.5 × BHW	2 × BHW	3 × BHW
Night-time shift			
20:00–22:00	1 × BHW	1.5 × BHW	2.5 × BHW
22:00–05:00	1.5 × BHW	2 × BHW	3 × BHW

Source: Bae, Kyuhan (1983: 58).

Note
BHW: Basic Hourly Wage.

extra work or overtime to boost total monthly working hours. For example, average monthly earnings of HMC production workers in 1983 were 355,000 won or about US$456, including bonus payments (Bae, Kyuhan 1983: 56–58). The average monthly earnings of other manufacturing workers in Korea at that time that ranged from 192 to 545,000 won (Bank of Korea 1983). However, given that overtime and bonus payments comprised 30 to 40 per cent of such earnings, it was necessary to work regular overtime and take extra jobs to reach an adequate income (Interview with HMC skilled worker 20 Jul. 1994). HMC thus manipulated its wages system to comply with the necessity of maintaining low-cost labour management and work intensification.

Until the late 1970s, company welfare systems scarcely existed. Even basic welfare facilities, such as subsidised meals, work uniforms, regular medical examinations, insurance for industrial accidents and the provision of public baths, were not well organised. Such basic welfare facilities as existed were mostly available only to professional managerial employees. However, since the development of large-scale mass production work organisation in the late 1970s, HMC has gradually built up its welfare facilities in order to promote the expansion of an internal labour market for professional managers. Various welfare programmes, such as housing support, educational scholarships for workers' children, leisure facilities for employees and their families, free medical check-ups, public baths and company bus services were developed over time.

Only basic facilities, such as dormitory accommodation and rest rooms to reduce the necessity for, and impact of, long-distance commuting were made available to production workers. The availability of facilities was further limited by the significant increases in employment of production workers during the late 1970s (HMC 1992: 464; Interview with an unionist 4 Aug. 1994).

Changes in employment relations policies and practices since the mid-1980s

One of the most significant changes in HMC's recruitment policy was that the informal practices of the 1970s were replaced by a formal ORS and recommendations by existing employees at the company level. From the late 1980s, the structure of the formal collective ORS for management group was also modified and augmented by the addition of written entrance examinations and interviews, as well as the development of an intern system, a recommendation system and a company and university cooperation system. The intern system was introduced in 1989 to facilitate the efficient recruitment of high-quality university graduates to the workforce by providing pre-selected candidates with indicative work experience in Hyundai and HMC during their vacation periods. The number of intern candidates so employed increased from 350 in 1989 to 564 in 1990 and 982 in 1992 at the Group level. On average, 70 to 80 per cent of intern candidates, or 10 to 20 per cent of total recruits, were subsequently hired under the ORS.

Selection was primarily undertaken on the basis of *curriculum vitae* assessment, written examination and interviews, regardless of employment class. Table 4.8

Table 4.8 Recruitment practices of HMC, 1980s-1990s

	Management candidate	*Production candidate*
Initiator	Group planning office	Personnel department at the factory level
Target	University graduates	High school graduates
age limit	up to 30	up to 35
Selection process		
Document assessment	Educational qualification, personal background	Education qualification, personal background
Written examination	Major, English	General knowledge, skill
Interview	Face to face group interview by top and personnel management	Face to face individual interview by head of respective department with personnel specialists

Sources: *Monthly Recruit* (Feb. 1987: 57, 61, Jul. 1987: 57, Oct. 1987, May 1990: 73); Hyorae *et al.* (1989); Hyundai Research Institute (Feb. 1990).

provides a simplified overview of the selection processes used by Hyundai in the 1980s and early 1990s. An age requirement was used to support HMC's seniority-based, hierarchical internal labour market, and written examinations were the key means of testing the knowledge and skills required for a particular job.

From the late 1980s, formalised selection processes have been gradually transformed with more emphasis being placed on individual contacts with potential recruits as well as face to face interviews in which interviewers rely on more qualitative techniques of assessment. For example, the technique of blind interviews was incorporated into the process of selecting university graduates to examine the attitudes of employees (Interview with HMC personnel specialist 10 Mar. 1999). The cultural values and beliefs, according to which candidates were assessed in interviews, included forethought, a positive attitude, thrift and collectiveness. Finally, in 1995, the pre-eminence of written examinations in the selection process was displaced by interviews.

From the mid-1980s, wage practices of HMC came under a serious challenge from its independent trade union. The collective bargaining process replaced unilateral decision making by management, which was the case until 1987. After the emergence of trade unions in 1987, the wage rate increased sharply by 20 per cent in 1987, 30 per cent in 1988 and 28 per cent in 1989 in comparison with approximately 6 per cent between 1982 and 1986 (Park, Joonshik 1991: 235). These wage increases undermined HMC's cost competitiveness (Table 4.9).

The most important advance which occurred in HMC from the mid-1980s was the implementation of an extensive welfare system in response to the emergence of a mass trade union movement. Welfare costs to HMC sharply increased from 286 billion won in 1986 to 604 billion won in 1988 and to 857 billion won in 1990. There was a causal connection between the development of company welfare programmes and the emergence of a trade union movement in 1987.

Table 4.9 Wage structure in HMC from the mid-1980s

TOTAL	(1) Monthly fixed wages	(1) Normal wage	(a) Basic wage
			(b) Allowances
		(2) Others allowance	(a) Other fixed allowance
			(b) Variable allowance
	(2) Other wages	(1) Bonus	
		(2) Superannuation	
	(3) Value added wages	(1) Performance	
		(2) Property wage	

Sources: Derived from internal sources of various wage structure tables of HMC in 1993, 1994, HGTUA (1994: 79, 1993: 106).

Note
Allowances: position, service years, dispatch, welfare, productivity improvement, risky work, shift work, harmful work, fixed overtime, family.

Various cultural programmes were organised in conjunction with training programmes and other employment activities at HMC in an effort to build a unitarist ideology of loyalty to the firm and to transform the anti-management sentiments held by many production workers. Welfare benefits, which until the early 1980s were limited to those in management, were extended to most production workers. A range of programmes and facilities, such as scholarships for the children of employees and company housing benefits, were achieved by the trade unions in their negotiations with HMC management.

Company-based welfare was one of the central issues in collective bargaining, due to the lack of a state welfare system in Korea. HMC and the trade unions established a joint project team to initiate and then manage a range of welfare programmes and facilities. For example, in 1990, HMC management and trade unions set up the *Employee Housing Construction Implementation Committee* to build houses for production workers (HMC 1992: 724; Kim, Wangun 1993: 303).

Labour-management relations at HMC, 1968–2000

Unlike other Hyundai subsidiary companies, such as HECC and HHI, workers in HMC appeared to be less militant and more compliant to management until the mid-1980s. One explanation of their quiescence was that despite strict supervision of labour management at HMC, the company developed a more 'rational' approach to the management of its production workers. For example, compared with HHI and HECC, HMC workers enjoyed relatively secure employment conditions due to the promotion of an internal labour market. This was due in part to HMC's desire to establish a mass production system in automobile manufacturing which required a stable workforce. HMC's workers suffered less from Hyundai management's work intensification policy in the 1970s, which was used in other subsidiary companies within HECC and HHI. Despite grievances over employment conditions and their working environment, auto workers at HMC had no choice but to accept management's authority as there were no alternative employers in the 1970s in the Ulsan Industrial Estate. In addition, HMC workers had witnessed the failure of strikes elsewhere and the punishment meted out to strikers by both repressive employers and the state (Bae, Kyuhan 1983: 76, 83, 104; Interviews with HECC foremen 3 Jul. 1994).

After these two serious industrial strikes at the Hyundai, however, the state and Hyundai management undertook to establish a resolution mechanism for industrial conflicts and to head off the trade union movement. The Labour Management Council (LMC) was established at the workplace in the 1970s. The LMC initially played a minimal role. Little occurred until 1980 when the new military government of Chun Doowhan endorsed LMCs with its *Labour Management Council Act*. The LMCs equal numbers of management and production worker representatives, as required by the *Act*. The LMCs in HMC were organised in accordance with the factory structure. Until the early 1980s, issues covered by the LMC were basically employment and welfare systems but they achieved little except minimal improvements in public baths and canteens, and with dormitory maintenance. In the early 1980s, however, welfare coverage was extended to issues such as productivity and wages by the new military government (Park, Funku 1982: 439, 446; Bae, Kyuhan 1983: 133; HHI 1992: 690, 712–713).

The LMC remained a limited institution because of its subordination to management and the state. The system was state-initiated without recognition of trade unions. Organisational function was technically subordinated to the state and management to solve labour issues in their favour.[12] The LMC's function was minimal, covering basic welfare matters or productivity improvement and excluding fundamental issues such as job security and wage increases. Hence, the LMC system was largely ignored by production workers. In 1982, 67 per cent of HMC's workers surveyed were not satisfied with the function or coverage of LMC activities and requested that they be expanded. The LMC was not seen as an adequate substitute for a genuine trade union (Bae, Kyuhan 1983: 104, 133; Interview with an HMC unionist 4 Aug. 1994).

Despite sufficient preconditions for the establishment of an organised labour movement in HMC, such as large-scale workforce and strict supervision, it did not emerge until the mid-1980s. This can be largely attributed to strength of the close economic ties between the state and the family-owned large conglomerates, or *chaebol*, including the Hyundai Business Group. This led the *chaebol* to adopt a repressive corporatist approach to the labour movement in furtherance of the objective of rapid economic growth underpinned by low labour costs. As the economic position of the *chaebol* became increasingly important for achieving high growth for the domestic economy, the state became more interventionist in workplace industrial relations, supporting the powers of the *chaebol*. Therefore, state-initiated industrial relations systems, such as the LMC, were top-down in their application. Because of its policy of maintaining low labour costs and maximising labour intensification, Hyundai and HMC implemented makeshift labour-management policies to weaken workforce resistance and enable them to remain competitive and expand rather than promote workplace industrial democracy. At the same time, Hyundai and the state used disruption to control labour directly. For example, those workers who were actively involved in the labour movement were expelled from the workplace. The fragility of the labour movement in Hyundai was also maintained by the state control of the national trade union organisation, Federation of Korean Trade Unions. As a result, workers became quiescent and obedient rather than be expelled from their workplace (Choi 1989; Kwon and O'Donnell 1999).[13]

The emergence of an independent trade union movement engendered a hostile response from Hyundai and HMC management which sought to annihilate it by various means such as the establishment of company unions, or physical violence and intimidation. Management opposition to the new trade unions was especially evident in HMC and HHI due largely to their dominant position within the Hyundai Group. To undermine and counteract the influence of the first independent trade union, management in HMC and HHI organised company-backed unions in 1987 with the support of pro-management production workers under the auspices of the Metal Federation of the Federation of Korean Trade Unions (FKTU). These unionists were mostly representatives of the LMCs and were regarded as labour aristocrats because of their corrupt relationship with management in the past (*Shin Dong-A* Jul. 1988: 382–395, Feb. 1989: 468–481).[14]

Before the changes to the Trade Union Act after 1987, the establishment of a company-backed union by management in any workplace, even without formal recognition by the FKTU, was a significant obstacle to the independent union movement obtaining legal status. The first task of an independent union was to obtain legal recognition in the workplace before it could combat management's unlawful labour practices. However, the newly emergent independent unions were needed to control the pent-up frustration of their members. After decades of suppression, numerous claims were made by workers – from the abolition of hair length regulations to the removal of unfair or discriminatory employment practices. In this tumultuous transitional period of Korea's political economy, it was not uncommon for workers' protests to assume an extreme form, including riots and aggressive street rallies. Furthermore, the trade unions faced with difficulties in bargaining with management as important local management decisions were subject to the central control of Hyundai senior management at the Group level. Hence, attempts to initiate collective bargaining processes at the local company level were often blocked by Hyundai top management.

To overcome the limitations of dealing with management on a local and individual workplace level, and build a strategic solidarity of trade unions across individual company boundaries, a cooperative trans-company organisation, Hyundai Group Trade Union Association (HGTUA) was founded on 8 August 1987. Two major unions, the HMC and HHI Trade Unions, were the central forces in HGTUA because of their membership size and the central production positions at Hyundai workplaces. The trade union movement in Hyundai was thus able to expand its coverage from the workplace level, to the entire organisation of the Hyundai Business Group. Even so, the function of HGTUA was confined to that of supporting the collective bargaining practices of affiliated unions at the workplace, due to the refusal by Hyundai top management to recognise its existence; in any case there were legal restrictions on the intervention of a 'third party' in workplace industrial relations by the Trade Union Act (*Monthly Mal* Mar. 1988; *Monthly Chosun* Aug. 1993: 188–199).

In relation to the peak bodies of HMC Trade Union, there was a distinction as to whether trade unions were affiliated to the HGTUA, the Korean Council of Trade Unions (KCTU) or the FKTU, depending on whether they were independent or company-oriented unionists. This happened in the early stage in the development of the trade union movement, post-1987. However, since the early 1990s, a strong relationship has emerged between the HGTUA and KCTU, as the leadership of the HMC Trade Union has been mostly ruled by independent trade unionists in HMC. As mentioned earlier, the HGTUA functioned as an upper body of Hyundai trade unions in the context of absence of a national union body of independent trade unions. However, the KCTU was formally organised in 1995 and HMC Trade Union was affiliated with the FMWU of the KCTU as a part of the industrial unionism policy of the KCTU in 1997. Hence, the HMC Trade Union became the central force in the FMWU and KCTU. For example, the former president of the HMC Trade Union became the president of KCTU in 1997 (Interview with HGTUA officer 9 Jun. 1994; FMWU senior officers 27–28 Mar. 1999; HMC Trade Union officer 30 Mar. 1999).

Because of the central role played by independent unionists in the HMC and the Hyundai trade union movement after 1987, direct management strategies were implemented to expel such unionists from their workplaces both on the grounds of claiming various unlawful actions and by institutional means. Until the early 1990s, terror tactics and violence were commonly used by HMC to disrupt the activities of the independent unions.

HMC management also encouraged company-backed unionists to take over control of trade union organisations through various dubious means. One example was the indirect involvement in the election of the union president using management-backed workers. This intervention brought about a split in the trade union movement at HMC and in HGTUA, between the HMC-backed unions and other independent unions, such as HHI Trade Union, which weakened their solidarity. In line with such strategy, management also developed a range of cultural and educational programmes which contained anti-union material or themes. Another example was HMC's anti-communist educational programmes which promoted an overlapping and equation of the 'red-menace' with independent unionists. In the course of such educational programmes, independent unionists were often described by lecturers as communists or disrupters (*Monthly Mal* Nov. 1987: 41; Interview with a former HMC Trade Union officer 2 Apr. 1999). Following changes to industrial relations legislation however, HMC was required to negotiate with the unions over the wages and conditions of its employees. The new era of labour relations thus required a new strategy to be developed by HMC.

Conclusion

This chapter has attempted to shed light on HMC's development as a major competitor in both the Korean and global automobile industries. It traced the emergence of the company from its modest origins as an automobile repair shop in 1946 to a global automobile manufacturer in 2000. The main impetus for its initial development was the Korean government's strategy of establishing the automobile industry, along with the shipbuilding and chemical industries, as a key element in the country's rapid industrialisation.

Although HMC began in partnership with the Ford Motor Company, and gained technical and financial assistance from Mitsubishi in its early stages of development, it has remained a family-owned *chaebol*. With the support of Mitsubishi, HMC produced its first original model, the *Pony*, in 1976. The model's success made HMC the leading automobile manufacturer in Korea and, by the end of the 1970s, HMC had captured more than half of the Korean automobile market. With the rapid expansion of its production capacity, HMC went on to develop a variety of other models. During the 1980s, HMC expanded its international sales and established a presence in North America, Turkey, India, China and Malaysia. However, in the latter part of that decade, domestic and international factors led to a loss of competitiveness. In response to this crisis, HMC developed a long-term business strategy to become one of the top ten automobile manufacturers in the world by 2000. In the course of implementing this strategy, HMC was severely affected by the Asian economic crisis of the late 1990s but survived by reducing production and accepting FDI. HMC emerged as the strongest Korean automobile company after the crisis and revived its plans for global manufacturing by expanding its operations in India and constructing new plants in the United States, China, Indonesia and Brazil.

In order to explain the success of HMC as an emerging global automobile company, this chapter has traced the development of HMC's manufacturing strategy from its initial CKD stage to mass production in the 1980s and 1990s. HMC's early alliance with Ford led to the development of a 'Fordist' assembly line as the model for the company's production system. The success of the *Pony* led to the establishment of a mass production system and prompted HMC to convert its production process from manual and small-scale assembly to mechanised large-scale assembly. Mitsubishi was also influential in providing technological support and training, as well as production equipment and machines. The influence of Mitsubishi led HMC to incorporate elements of a Japanese approach to labour management, particularly quality management techniques, which yielded significant production cost savings. Since the mid-1980s, production has expanded as a result of technological changes. The introduction of industrial robots in the mid-1980s facilitated automation and mechanisation of production lines.

The success of HMC's manufacturing strategy, which enabled it to produce more than one million vehicles per year at its Ulsan complex by the early 1990s, has been closely linked to its employment relations policies and practices. The Korean government's prohibition on trade union organisations until 1987 enabled management to unilaterally determine the wages and conditions of employees. This resulted in HMC achieving massive increases in production while holding wages low and intensifying work practices. However, it was not until the mid-1970s that an expanding workforce under mass production forced HMC to establish an internal labour market and formalise its previously *ad hoc* approach to employment relations. Wage schemes were also developed in this period to support a seniority-based labour market which incorporated a basic wage plus various allowances.

Perhaps the greatest impetus for change in employment relations at HMC was the emergence of the trade union movement. After 1987, HMC was under pressure to improve the wages and welfare of its employees. Faced with growing militancy from its previously compliant workforce, and an independent union movement, HMC reacted with hostility and sought to establish its own company union. However, the HMC union became a key force within the newly formed peak council, the Korean Council of Trade Unions (KCTU), and ultimately gained recognition from the Korean government under the new labour legislation. HMC therefore had to come to terms with a new environment in which unions had stronger legislated rights. Although the economic crisis in 1997 caused unions to make wage concessions in order to retain jobs in the industry and the government eased restrictions against lay-offs and redundancies, HMC is now required to engage with unions in a collective bargaining process. Wage increases and the implementation of an extensive welfare system have undermined HMC's competitiveness, which has traditionally been based on a policy of maintaining low labour costs and intensification of work. The future development of HMC as a global automobile manufacturer will therefore depend upon its ability to come to terms with demands by its employees and their unions for improved wages and conditions, not only in Korea but also in its overseas plants, such as Chennai.

5 Production systems and supplier relations

Introduction

As outlined in previous chapters, Hyundai Motor Company (HMC) entered the Indian passenger car market in 1996 by establishing a wholly-owned subsidiary company, Hyundai Motors India (HMI). Construction on the greenfield site, just outside the city of Chennai, was completed in September 1999. The plant was built with a capacity to manufacture 120,000 passenger cars per annum. Some 80,000 units of this capacity was for the manufacture of the 999cc *Santro* and 40,000 units for the more powerful 1499cc *Accent*. The *Santro* was HMI's inaugural model and was targeted at the mid-size range of the Indian passenger vehicle market. Apart from a larger engine, this model was equivalent to HMC's *Atoz* in the Korean market. In August 1999, HMI launched its second passenger car, the *Accent*. Again, this car had an equivalent model produced by HMC for the Korean market, the *Verna*.

Thus far, it appears that HMI's entry into the Indian automobile market has been successful. After only 14 months, HMI began to make profits. By May 2000, production output exceeded 100,000 passenger cars. Accordingly, HMI's market share had grown rapidly from its initial entry into the Indian market in late 1998. In its first year of production, HMI accounted for only 2.2 per cent of the market. This figure climbed significantly to 11 per cent in 1999 and to 14 per cent in 2000. At the same time, Toyota–Maruti, the dominant local auto maker (a joint venture between Toyota and Maruti, a national corporation of India), was losing ground with market share declining from 82 per cent in 1998 to 55 per cent in 2000.

HMI quickly became one of the fastest growing automobile manufacturers in India's fiercely competitive market. In the mid-range passenger vehicle market, eight models from six manufacturers compete for market share. HMI's *Santro* achieved a market share of 24 per cent. This placed HMI only slightly behind the market leader, Maruti, whose equivalent model held 25 per cent of the market share. During the first quarter of 2000, HMI's *Accent* achieved market leadership in the premium product class with sales of 6,223 cars, or 20 per cent of this market segment. By contrast, Ford, which had previously been the largest supplier, sold 6,182 during the same period, slightly behind HMI's sales.

The successful entry of HMI into the Indian automobile market was well supported by efficient and effective management of production at the Chennai plant. The production figures outlined in the following table demonstrate

HMC's success in transporting its production systems from Korea to India. This success has underpinned rapid growth in the Indian market in a relatively short timeframe. Table 5.1 shows the increase in HMI's production output since 1998 and reveals that although HMI's production efficiency was quite erratic during the first four months of production, it quickly stabilised.

HMI production strategy and management

This section examines HMI's product strategy and production management practices. HMI's successful entry into the Indian market largely depended on its ability to produce higher quality models at a lower cost than its competitors. As such, the driving force of the various elements of HMI's production management practices embodied a high-quality, low-cost strategy. This chapter will explore the variety of methods adopted by HMI to maximise product quality, while simultaneously containing the overall cost of production. Comparisons will be made with the strategy of HMC in Korea. The relationship between product strategy and production is also analysed. The link with employment relations is examined in Chapter 6.

The timing of the move into the Indian automobile industry saw HMI as a late market entrant. To support the move, HMI launched the same models in both the Indian and Korean markets. HMI's *Accent* began production in August 1999 and was launched at the same time as its equivalent model in Korea, the *Verna*. This simultaneous launching of new products in different countries contrasts with the product launching strategy of other multinational auto makers in India. Generally, automobiles produced in India were at least one model behind the equivalent model of the country of origin. This practice was developed as a way for multinational auto makers to use passenger vehicle markets in developing countries as a 'dumping ground' for lower priced, older models. It also limited the market price of new cars in developing countries. This approach meant that, in order to compete, HMI needed to price its products to be responsive to local market conditions.

The price positioning of HMI's two models in the Indian market clearly demonstrated the low-cost policy discussed earlier. In May 2000, the price for mid-range passenger vehicle products (where HMI's *Santro* was located) ranged from between 220,000 and 483,463 rupees. The *Santro* sold for between 315,500 and 379,500 rupees. In the case of the premium product market (in which the *Accent* competed), prices varied from 472,574 to 985,739 rupees. The *Accent* sold for between 541,000 and 591,000 rupees. Both HMI cars were clearly targeted towards the lower end of the price range within their respective product markets. HMI aimed to satisfy both the goals of cost competitiveness and quality enhancement.

Production technologies and production processes at HMI and HMC

The mass production system utilised by HMI in Chennai for the *Santro* and the *Accent* was based on assembly line processes initially developed at HMC's Ulsan

Table 5.1 Monthly production trends at HMI Chennai, 1998–2000

		Month										
		08/98	*09/98*	*10/98*	*11/98*	*12/98*	*01/99*	*02/99*	*03/99*	*04/99*	*05/99*	*06/99*
Body	Units produced	98	905	1,594	2,850	3,828	3,098	3,000	3,337	3,516	4,682	4,834
	efficiency %	16.3	22.2	40.8	68.6	91.9	91.4	74.4	69.0	75.0	90.1	87.9
Assembly	Units produced	11	786	1,430	2,924	3,751	3,150	3,024	3,352	3,482	4,634	4,802
	efficiency %	6.4	9.2	38.0	69.5	90.3	93.3	83.4	79.3	82.6	98.1	98.5

		Month									
		07/99	*08/99*	*09/99*	*10/99*	*11/99*	*12/99*	*01/00*	*02/00*	*03/00*	*04/00*
Body	Units produced efficiency %	4,237	6,902	7,512	6,465	6,751	7,562	7,381	7,654	8,230	7,097
		86.3	88.9	93.2	82.2	82.3	85.1	89.9	89.6	89.2	86.6
Assembly	Units produced efficiency %	4,177	6,998	7,416	6,463	9,762	7,588	7,343	7,658	8,201	7,109
		93.4	98.9	95.5	90.5	90.7	94.0	98.3	98.6	97.8	95.4

Source: HMI (1999–2000c).

Note
Units produced: Santro and Accent models only; Accent has been produced since August in 1999.

plant. HMC has a production capacity of 500,000 units per annum for its two equivalent models. HMC built the Chennai plant and designed its production system along similar lines to the Ulsan plant, where the *Atoz* and *Accent* were produced. In the Ulsan plant, a limited flexible mass production system was developed which produced a number of similar models on the same production line. This concept was applied to the Chennai plant, which was also designed to assemble multiple units, namely the *Santro* and the *Accent*, using the same production process.

Although both plants utilise similar mass production concepts, there remain considerable differences in production technologies and processes between the Chennai and Ulsan plants. HMI's production systems were more labour intensive and utilised more semi-mechanised processes. By contrast, the HMC plant in Ulsan placed greater reliance on automation. These differences reflect the different local conditions faced by both companies in their respective local labour markets. To maximise cost competitiveness, labour-intensive assembly was preferred by HMI as this enabled the Chennai plant to take full advantage of a relatively low-paid and lower-skilled local workforce in comparison with Korea. The emphasis on mechanisation and automation is explained by the higher labour costs experienced by HMC, whose workers are organised into an independent enterprise union at the Ulsan plant. Reliance on labour-intensive production was also adopted by HMI for political reasons. When it entered the Indian market, HMI was lobbied by the state government to maximise the size if its workforce in a labour market and society characterised by high levels of unemployment. In response to these pressures, production equipment was installed to maximise the labour-intensive nature of the production process at the Chennai plant.

The *Santro* and *Accent* were initially designed and assembled using HMC's highly automated and mechanised production lines in Korea, fully supported by HMC's advanced quality management techniques. While HMI relied on labour-intensive assembly in combination with semi-mechanised production lines to contain production costs, it was also imperative for HMI management to narrow the gap in quality between the HMI and HMC models. HMI placed considerable emphasis on improving product quality to achieve a similar level to that at HMC whilst maintaining a focus on efficiency and cost competitiveness.

Structure of production processes

Basic characteristics of the production process

HMI's plant was organised into five main shops – press/body, paint, assembly, engine and transmission. Initially, in October 1998, HMI employed 1,400 workers. In August 1999, this figure increased to 2,290 workers operating on a two-shift system. The number of employees increased again by January 2001 to 3,000 with the plant operating on a three-shift production system.

HMI's production processes were partly automated, semi-mechanised and labour intensive. As seen in Figure 5.1, there were two independent floor and side

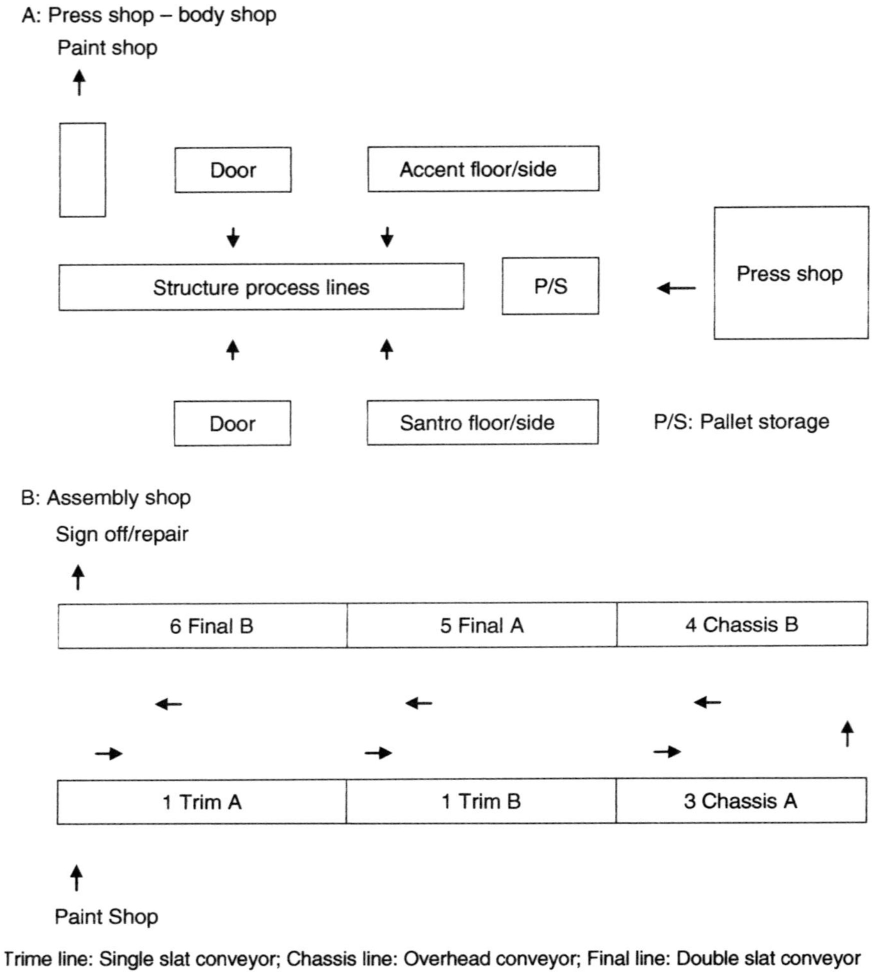

Figure 5.1 Production process structure of HMI.

Sources: HMC (1998–2001c); HMI (1999–2000c).

lines and one united production line. Once a basic pallet of the product was produced by the press shop, it was then delivered to the body shop. Depending on the model, the pallet was then delivered to either the *Accent* or the *Santro* floor and side lines. The finished product then flowed onto a united production line from the press shop to the painting and assembly shop. The production line was designed to produce one *Accent* for every three *Santros*.

The production process structure, outlined in Figure 5.1, involved the production of multiple models in a mass production system, and was originally developed by HMC. In HMC's Korean production facilities, a Flexible Body Line

System (FBLS) was installed in the press and body shops in order to produce four different models concurrently. These followed through into one united mass production process. The main difference between the production processes at HMC and HMI was the extent of automation and mechanisation. In HMI, production lines in the press and front part of the body shop were organised by a number of models as outlined in Figure 5.1. By contrast, similar parts of production lines in the press and body shop of HMC were organised with the full utilisation of machinery and automation systems. This was largely attributed to the steep rise in labour costs at HMC in the aftermath of the emergence of an independent trade union movement in the post-1987 period. Although the manufacture of multiple products in a mass production system was also applied to the HMI plant, the company needed to minimise production costs. Hence, different models for different production lines were installed in the Press and front part of body shop to minimise the high cost of introducing mechanised and automated systems and to maximise the utilisation of HMI's workforce.

Production process management

The increased utilisation of labour by HMI is shown by analysing overall production stations and operations. Table 5.2 details the structure of the production process of the body and assembly shops in the Chennai plant including the number of substations and staffing levels. The body shop production lines were organised into 142 substations with 131 workers (0.92 workers per substation) while the assembly shop production lines were organised into 162 substations with 86 workers (0.53 workers per substation) to produce a maximum of 120,000 units. In contrast to this structure, HMC's more automated production lines relied on fewer workers per substation. For example, the first production line of the body shop in the Ulsan plant engaged 259 substations with 174 workers (0.67 workers per substation) and produced 310,000 units of the *Verna* model.

There were also considerable differences between the number of robots used in the Chennai and Ulsan plants. In Chennai, only nine robots were used in the press and body shops and only 188 semi-auto spot welding guns were allocated to achieve 22 units per hour. By contrast, the Ulsan plant utilised 257 robots to achieve 75 units per hour. The semi-auto spot welding guns were phased out in the Ulsan plant and replaced with fully automated spot welding guns.

HMI's approach to production technology was therefore indicative of a production management strategy focused on minimising production costs and maximising the utilisation of its relatively low-paid local labour force.

The main characteristics of HMI's and HMC's production systems, which resulted in equivalent models, are shown in Table 5.3. The data demonstrate the labour-intensive nature of HMI's production systems whereby, on average, 3.6 workers were assigned to a substation in contrast to HMC's average of 2.2 and 1.9 workers in the first and second factory in Ulsan. This highlights the greater reliance by HMC on automation. The data also reveal that although HMI maintained a more labour-intensive and less mechanised production system, the production line maintained approximately the same speed as that of HMC's first

Table 5.2 Production process structure of the body and assembly shop of HMI by number of substations and workers, August 1999 – April 2000

Body shop				*Assembly shop*		
Line	*Model*	*Substations*	*Workers*	*Line*	*Substations*	*Workers*
Main lines				*Main lines*		
Floor	Santro	26	26	Trim A	13	20
	Accent	17	12	Trim B	10	14
Side	Santro	23	21	Chassis A	7	7
	Accent	25	11	Chassis B	5	7
Body build	Together	16	24	Final A	15	20
Moving	Together	16	18	Final B	12	9
	Together	10	7	Keepers	N/A	9
Body complete	Together	9	12			
Sub-total		142	131	Sub-total	162	86
Average				Average		
Sub-lines				*Sub-lines*		
Fuel Tank	Together	9	3	Tire/glass	2	6
Relief	Together	N/A	10	First structure	1	2
Jig	Together	N/A	4	Fuel tank/ tube	2	3
Tool room	Together	N/A	1	Sub-frame	1	2
Keeper	Together	N/A	3	Engine/ radiator	2	8
Sub-total		9	21	Sub-total	8	21
Total		142	152	Total/shift	170	107

Sources: HMC (1998–2001c); HMI (1999–2000a,c).

Notes

The body shop structure of production process is based 22 UPH and designed to flow 3 Santro units and 1 Accent unit in the line.

The Assembly Shop structure of production process is based 20 UPH. 1 UPH = 1 output/per hour; UPL = a number of units on the production lines during operation of production lines.

factory in Ulsan. This implies that HMI was successful in maximising the utilisation of its workforce. This was a considerable achievement given the short period of time that the greenfield site had been in operation.

The basic unit of labour process and skill formation

The labour-intensive nature of production processes at the Chennai plant was evident when comparing the production and labour processes for a substation at both the Chennai and Ulsan plants. Figure 5.2 highlights the differences in production processes between the two plants. In the case of the central floor assembly re-spot station C of the Chennai plant, all three workers were in charge of assembling parts and welding spots using semi-auto welding guns. By contrast,

Table 5.3 Major characteristics of assembly shops in HMI and first and second plant of HMC in Ulsan, 1999

	Company		
	HMI	*HMC 1*	*HMC 2*
Production capacity	120,000 units	100,000 units	200,000 units
Model	Santro/Accent	Accent	Atoz and alike
Conveyor			
Total length	570	623	900
No. of stations	82	100	113
UPL	100	120	150
Process time	5	5	3.75
Speed	1.8m/min.	2.0 m/min.	3.6 m/min.
Station pitch	5.4	6.0	6
Operational UPH	20 UPH	20 UPH	40 UPH
Manpower			
Direct	266	182	188
Indirect	28	38	28
Manpower/per station	3.58	2.2	1.91

Sources: HMC (1998–2001b,c); HMI (1999–2000c).

Notes
1UPH = 1 output/ per hour; UPL = a number of units on the production lines during operation of production lines.

in the equivalent substation of the Ulsan plant, four robots were installed at four angles. HMI relied on labour-intensive production utilising a low-skilled workforce whilst seeking to maintain the quality levels found at the Ulsan factories. Achieving this goal required a combination of efficient production practices and strict control over the low-skilled workforce.

Figure 5.2 demonstrates how HMI applied a scientific approach to organising its production processes. The process separated the complicated production process into a number of simplified and fragmented sub-production processes. Hyundai had long experience of utilising this approach in its automobile manufacturing operations in Korea. However, this approach involved a process of de-skilling whereby complicated production tasks were re-organised into a number of repetitive and simplified tasks. It involved dividing production lines into a number of substations and assigning workers to jobs that were fragmented, simplified and precisely timed. Table 5.4 indicates how each worker was required to finish within a given time period and in accordance with prescribed methods and using particular production tools. The equivalent work station at the Ulsan plant was replaced by robots, outlined in Figure 5.2.

HMI's scientific approach maximised the utilisation of a relatively cheap and lower-skilled local workforce. As the job tasks undertaken by workers in the HMI production process were fragmented into simple tasks, it was much easier to train and allocate unskilled production workers within the assembly lines at short notice. This is evident in the training programmes for new production workers. Once workers were recruited, they received a two-day orientation programme which

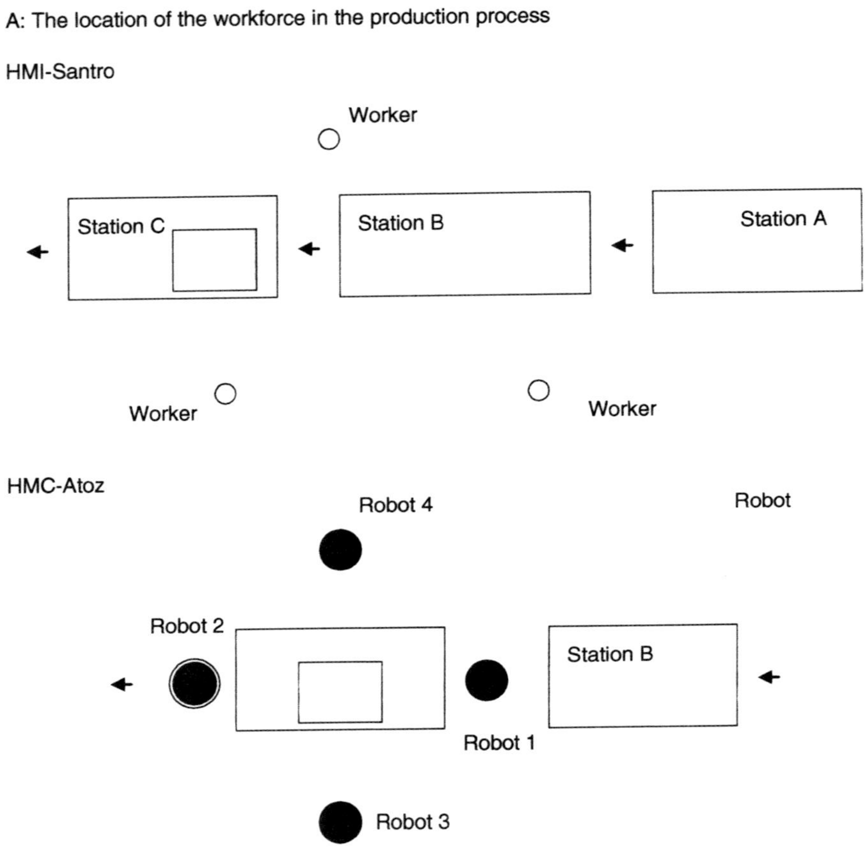

Figure 5.2 The labour process, in the case of central floor assembly re-spot Station C, in the body shop of both HMI and HMC.

Sources: HMC (1998–2001c); HMI (1999–2000c).

focused mainly on introducing them to HMI. They were then assigned to particular production lines and spent two weeks undergoing on-the-job training as 'assistant workers' overseen by both their supervisors and more senior employees.

Once the production lines stabilised from mid-1999, HMI introduced a job rotation system which allowed production workers to periodically change jobs. This scheme was aimed at reducing fatigue and monotony for the workers as well as facilitating multi-skilling. The ultimate goal was an increase in productivity. Once workers completed a less-skilled, tedious job for a period of 15 days, they were then assigned to undertake a higher-skilled job in order to avoid fatigue or the risks associated with tedious and/or dangerous tasks. Figure 5.3 shows the operation of the job rotation system. Newly recruited technicians in the assembly

Table 5.4 Station work description and process (HMI and HMC)

HMI (Santro)				*HMC (Atoz)*			
Work description	*Welding points*	*Tool*	*Standard time (sec)*	*Work description*	*Welding points*	*Tool*	*Standard time (sec)*
Work in Station B			115.73	Part loading		Shuttle	11
Move to Station C		3 workers	4.13	Clamp			1.5
Check specification			1.56	Welding			31.0
Spot(hand) welding		Portable gun	71.69	Welding 1	12 pts	Robot 1	(31.0)
Left hand	16 pts			Welding 2	12 pts	Robot 2	(31.0)
Right hand	26 pts			Welding 3	10 pts	Robot 3	(31.0)
Unclamp			2	Welding 4	10 pts	Robot 4	(31.0)
Return to Station B		3 workers	(4.13)	Unclamp			1.5

Sources: HMC (1998–2001b,c); HMI (1999–2000c).

shop were not allowed to participate in the job rotation system until they had completed three months of employment at HMI.

Production improvement activities

A Quality Department was established from the outset at HMI. It comprised 152 workers organised into 5 teams (one for each of the main shops) and was responsible for the maintenance of product quality in each production line sector. The Department's role was to oversee all inputs into the production lines from initial parts and semi-finished products. The Department inspected production equipment and machinery used in the course of the production process. The goal of the Department was to prevent default problems arising during the operation of production. In addition, the Department was responsible for promoting a range of productivity improvement activities including job suggestion schemes and quality circle activities. All of these activities were transplanted from HMC's Ulsan plants, although they were not fully utilised at the Chennai plant, at least in the early stages of the plant's operation.

By late 2000, however, the Quality Department began to implement a job suggestion scheme in earnest. It was introduced to improve quality, reduce production costs and to enhance employees' attitudes to work. The system was devised in order to motivate participants through a combination of financial and cultural award systems. It provided monthly financial payments of between 4,000 and 5,000 rupees. Table 5.5 outlines the success of the Department's activities and demonstrates that the number of complaints from *Santro* buyers declined from 11 per cent of total sales in January 1999 to 2 per cent in March 2000.

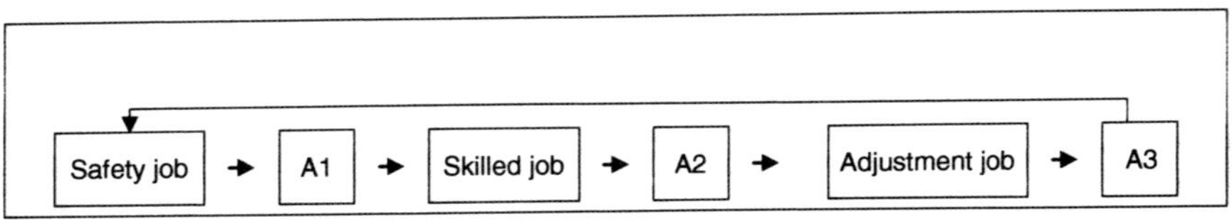

Figure 5.3 The job rotation process of HMI.

Source: HMI (1999–2000c).

Note
A = tedious, hazardous, heavy and general jobs.

Table 5.5 Complaint trend by sales of HMI Santro, 1999–2000

	Month							
	01/99	*03/99*	*05/99*	*07/99*	*09/99*	*11/99*	*01/00*	*03/00*
Total no. of complaints	341	384	378	345	384	231	238	131
Sales	3,078	3,344	4,218	4,824	7,315	6,235	6,085	6,298
% complaints/sales	11.0	11.5	9.0	7.2	5.2	3.7	3.9	2.1

Source: HMI (1999–2000c).

In comparison with the role of HMI's Quality Department (where the focus was on preventing default problems and claims), the duties of the Quality Division at HMC were much wider and extended to the development of company policy in relation to quality improvement as well as its implementation at the workplace level. The Quality Division of the Ulsan Plant comprised 553 employees organised into six teams including planning, production technology, quality assurance, engine quality, transmission and testing. HMC's Quality Division was also in charge of a range of productivity improvement activities and systems. The emergence of independent trade unions at the Ulsan plant had a significant influence on the Division's activities. Workers came to view the financial payments made from the staff suggestion scheme as an important supplement to their base pay rather than reflecting employee acceptance of the goals of quality enhancement or productivity improvement. Table 5.6 demonstrates that the job suggestion scheme at HMC was less effective as a means of improving productivity. Although the number of suggestions increased substantially, the actual level of financial savings and the number of proposals selected for implementation declined.

Research and development

HMI's research and development (R&D) section was organised by two managers redeployed from HMC and one local employee. The R&D function at the HMI plant, however, was subordinated to the activities of HMC's R&D office. The research and development work undertaken by HMI consisted of gathering local information on particular car models and the circumstances of the Indian automobile industry generally, such as the types of quality issues that are relevant to the Indian environment. This information was then considered during the development of new models that HMI sought to launch in India. In addition, HMI's R&D section dealt with local government regulations affecting new model passenger cars and the paperwork involved in the acquisition of export licenses.

The supply chain

Developing an efficient parts supply system was of critical importance to successful production at the Chennai plant. Since the local automobile part

Table 5.6 Job suggestion system and quality circles status of HMC, 1997–1998

Year	*Suggestion*		*Quality circles*	
	No. of suggested proposals	*Saving amount*	*No. of selected proposals*	*Saving amount*
1997	333,310	589	3,390	177
1998	452,521	550	3,085	185

Sources: HMC (1998–2001b,c); HMI (1999–2000b,c).

Note
Unit: 100 million won.

suppliers were not providing the level of quality required, HMI initially brought in a range of Korean vendors who had considerable experience in supplying the HMC plant in Ulsan. Altogether, including joint ventures, some 13 Korean parts suppliers were organised in close proximity to the Chennai plant. However, production costs escalated with the imposition of sizeable tariffs by the Indian government on the importation of automobile parts. These tariffs were compounded by the high cost of exporting parts from Korea. Hence, HMI subsequently shifted to a policy of indigenisation, or local production and supply of automobile parts. As a result of this change of policy, the level of local auto parts supplied increased from 20 per cent in late 1998 to 65 per cent in early 2000.

Table 5.7 shows the indigenisation status of HMI's supply chain for auto parts. In India at this time, there were 65 different vendors supplying 1,280 automobile parts to HMI, representing 75 per cent of total automobile supply costs. Among them, 13 Korean vendors (including joint ventures) produced 874 parts or 49 per cent of total supply cost, while Indian vendors supplied 406 parts, or 24 per cent of total supply costs. The varying levels of supply, between Korean and Indian part suppliers, reflected the gap in production technologies between local and Korean vendors. This reliance by HMI on Korean part suppliers was in line with the company's emphasis on maximising product quality as an essential element of its entry strategy to the Indian market.

Table 5.8 further shows HMI's policy of quality management in its supply chain. This table illustrates the locale of supply of various key inputs. Steel board materials, that demanded high quality manufacturing processes, were imported directly from Korea, whereas aluminium materials available from the local producers were sourced from local Indian suppliers.

Table 5.9 shows the geographical proximity of HMI's automobile parts supply chain. Most Korean and joint venture operators were located within an hour's drive from the Chennai plant. Others, in particular local Indian part suppliers, were located a considerable distance from the plant. This was because most of India's manufacturing industries were located in the north of the country and Chennai is located in the South-Eastern corner. This geographical separation created unique difficulties for HMI as it attempted to establish an efficient parts supply chain that was responsive to sudden changes in demand and would ensure supplies arrived at the production lines in a timely manner.

HMI's lack of quality control over automobile part supplies during the early periods of production at Chennai resulted in a high level of customer complaints. As there was insufficient infrastructure for the automobile industry in Chennai, HMI encouraged Korean suppliers for HMC to relocate to the region. However, these vendors also faced serious production problems as they adjusted to the Indian environment. In addition, Indian suppliers often did not supply parts in the required timeframe nor to the level of quality required by HMI. These delays and quality problems resulted in frequent stoppages to HMI's main production lines at the Chennai plant. In response to these initial production difficulties, HMI expended considerable effort in developing a more reliable parts supply chain.

Table 5.7 Indigenisation of auto parts at HMI, 2000

Type	*No. of vendors*	*No. of parts supplied*			*Supply cost by total cost (per %)*		
		Santro	*Accent*	*Total*	*Santro*	*Accent*	*Total*
Local supplier							
Korean vendor	2	46	50	96	6	4	5
Joint venture	11	390	388	778	45	41	44
Total A	13	436	438	874	51	45	49
Multinational vendor	9	57	29	86	7	1	5
Indian vendors	43	177	143	320	21	13	19
Total B	52	234	172	406	28	14	24
Total C	65	670	610	1280	79	59	73
HMI		59	36	95	6	3	5
Total D	65	729	646	1375	85	62	79
Import from HMC		576	868	1444	15	38	21
Total		1,305	1,514	2,819	100	100	100

Source: HMI (1999–2000a,b,c).

Note
Joint venture implies a Korean vendor in partnership with a local Indian vendor.

Table 5.8 Location of supply of production material

Type	*Total (%)*	*Imported from Korea (%)*			*Obtained within India (%)*		
		Santro	*Accent*	***Total***	*Santro*	*Accent*	***Total***
Steel board materials	100	59	14	**73**	22	5	**27**
Plastic materials	100	0	15	**15**	71	14	**85**
Aluminium materials	100	0	0	**0**	75	25	**100**

Source: HMI (1999–2000b).

Table 5.9 Location of vendors by distance from HMI plant

Number of vendors	*Distance (km)*	*Delivery hours (hours)*
36	50	1
8	500	24
8	1,500	96
13	2,500	168
Total 65		

Source: HMI (1999–2000b).

Table 5.10 Stoppage analysis of HMI body shop, October 1999–February 2000

Problem type	*10/1999*		*12/1999*		*02/2000*	
	No.	*%*	*No.*	*%*	*No.*	*%*
Machine	156	3.5	16	0.4	154	6.2
Work shop	297	6.7	8	0.2	368	14.4
Part	1,400	31.7	1,672	44.0	11	0.7
Shuttle	52	1.2	4	0.1	59	2.4
Conveyor	78	1.8	0	0	16	0.6
Gun	431	9.8	63	1.7	185	7.4
Jig	46	1.0	1	0.0	59	2.4
Robot	147	3.3	9	0.2	148	6.0
Non-working hour	441	10.0	486	12.8	286	11.5
Other shop	619	14.0	94	2.5	63	2.5
Others	736	16.7	1,434	37.7	1,139	45.8
Total	4,410	100	3,796	100	2,486	100
Working days	23					

Source: HMI (1999–2000a,b,c).

This was largely achieved by 2000. Table 5.10 details the causes of production stoppages in 1999 and 2000. The table documents that some 1,400 stoppages occurred in October 1999 due to problems with parts supply. However, the number of stoppages had declined to 11 by February 2000.

Conclusion

This chapter has outlined the establishment of HMI's production systems in Chennai and the company's successful entry into the increasingly competitive Indian automobile market. The key to HMI's success in India has been its strategy to produce high-quality vehicles at a lower cost than its rivals. To achieve this goal, HMI based its production methods, strategies and management on HMC's Ulsan plant in Korea. Gradually, however, HMI is developing its own approach to meet the demands of the Indian labour force, automobile part suppliers and consumers.

The Chennai plant was designed and built along the lines of the Ulsan plant's system of flexible mass production, developed in Korea, which allows a number of similar models to be produced on the same production line. However, the Chennai plant is distinctive in that its semi-mechanised production systems are more labour intensive than the highly automated operations at the Ulsan plant. The principal reason for this difference is the comparatively low-paid and less-skilled Indian labour force, which has enabled HMI to contain its production costs in contrast to the higher labour costs of unionised workers at HMC in Ulsan. Low labour costs have also minimised the expense of introducing mechanised and automated production systems. Regardless of the differences between the labour markets, however, HMI has endeavoured to achieve the level of product quality similar to that of HMC.

Achieving the goal of high-quality vehicles at low cost has required efficient production practices combined with strict control over labour. HMI applied the principles of mass production to maximise the utilisation of its relatively low-skilled and low-cost workforce by fragmenting jobs into simplified and precisely timed tasks. Simplified tasks meant that it was easier for HMI to replace and train unskilled production workers on the assembly line in relatively brief periods of time. To offset the monotony and fatigue and to facilitate multi-skilling and productivity among its workforce, HMI introduced a job rotation system which allowed production workers who had completed more than three months at the plant to periodically change between lower- and higher-skilled jobs.

Further, in accordance with its emphasis on quality, HMI established a Quality Development Department. The Department comprised workers from each of the plant's main shops and its responsibilities ranged from process and product inspections to productivity improvement activities. A job suggestion scheme which used financial and cultural awards to motivate participants and improve employee attitudes was particularly successful, especially in comparison to the Quality Control Division at HMC which was more extensive in scope but less effective due to union opposition. HMI's research and development is more closely aligned with HMC. It comprises two HMC managers deployed to India and one local employee. While local issues are considered, HMI retains close ties to R&D at HMC.

The supply chain was initially sourced from Korean companies. Whilst the Korean component suppliers provided parts at the required standard to meet HMI's entry strategy as a high-quality producer, HMI has gradually switched to cheaper local production and supply of automobile parts. However, this process encountered several difficulties. The efficiency and responsiveness of the parts supply chain was affected by the geographical separation of HMI in South-Eastern India from the majority of manufacturing industries in the northern region. HMI received numerous customer complaints arising from their lack of quality control over parts from local suppliers. These quality problems, together with delays in the supply of parts, resulted in frequent stoppages of HMI's production lines. After considerable effort to increase the reliability and efficiency of its supply chain, stoppages had declined by 2000. Due to the labour-intensive nature of HMI's production systems, however, the success of the company has also been dependent on developing effective employment relations systems, which will be discussed in Chapter 6.

6 The management of employment relations

Introduction

The production processes and strategies outlined in Chapter 5 had a significant impact on employment relations practices at Hyundai Motors India (HMI). The rapid expansion in production capacity (an increase of 100,000 passenger cars per annum) subsequently resulted in rapid employment growth over a relatively short period of time. This too had a strong impact on employment relations at HMI.

HMI began production operations with a workforce of approximately 1,400 workers operating on a one-shift production system. By August 1999, the workforce had grown to 2,290 workers operating a two-shift system. The workforce continued to expand. By January 2001 there were approximately 3,000 workers operating a three-shift system. This expansion meant that HMI needed to develop a range of employment relations policies in order to effectively manage its workforce.

There are three key driving forces behind HMI's employment relations policies and practices. First, in response to its low-cost entry strategy, HMI needed to develop a cost efficient approach to its internal labour market arrangements. Second, HMI needed to recruit high-quality employees even though they aimed to minimise wage costs. Third, HMI sought to remain a non-unionised company and to avoid industrial unrest. In Korea, conflict between Hyundai Motor Company (HMC) and its enterprise trade union resulted in rising labour costs and reduced competitiveness. HMI's employment relations strategy was to minimise the potential for industrial disputes by avoiding unions.

This chapter will explore the variety of employment relations methods adopted by HMI to enhance its product market position and thereby maximise the efficiencies arising from its labour-intensive operations.

Organisational structure and hierarchy

HMI's initial task was to formalise its employment relations policies in response to the rapid growth in workforce numbers. To do this, HMI adopted a dual internal labour market approach that differentiated between managerial and production employees in relation to wages, promotion and welfare facilities. The dual labour market began at the entry point and was based on different educational requirements.

HMI's management hierarchy was organised into six grades from the most senior management position down to those working on the production line. This hierarchy was divided into three clusters. The first cluster was the management group comprised of workshop senior managers (such as team leaders, production controllers and mainline controllers). These managerial employees were normally recruited from the available pool of engineering university graduates (a six-year degree). The second cluster were the cell leaders (or junior engineers), who functioned at the middle level of the managerial hierarchy and who were recruited from the available pool of technology college graduates (two-year trained). These employees played a key role in controlling particular sectors of the main production lines. The final cluster comprised sub-cell keepers (or senior technicians) and production line workers. These workers were recruited from the available pool of high school graduates. The line working group was organised into groups of between 8 and 12 workers. Formal education qualifications, therefore, created clear demarcations between the different levels of the employment hierarchy at HMI.

Figure 6.1 provides an outline of HMI's organisational structure for production operations at the Chennai plant and includes the management structure at workshop level. As explained in Chapter 5, passenger car production was organised into five shops (press/body, paint, assembly, engine and transmission). Other departments, such as management, quality control, maintenance and utilities were created to support these main production lines. This structure was similar to that which existed at HMC's Ulsan operation. One key difference however, was that HMC's production planning and controlling units were not found in the Chennai plant. Rather, the office for overseas production technologies at the Ulsan plant of HMC carried out these functions. This meant that the role of HMI's production division was simply to adjust its production to the requirements of the local Indian market. At the workshop level, as demonstrated in Figure 6.1, five hierarchical grades were developed to undertake production operations.

Table 6.1 shows the evolution of HMI's internal labour market structure. In 1999, 25 positions were divided between executive and non-executive groups. The executive group was organized into an 11 step hierarchy while the non-executive group consisted of 14 production worker positions.

In May 2000, this employment structure was further sub-divided into four groups: 10 executive positions, 4 junior executive positions, 4 junior engineer and 9 production worker positions. The hierarchy also expanded from 25 to 27 positions in response to the rapid expansion in the workforce. However, the new structure created conflict among the different groups as promotion was the key to enhancing both social status as well as income. The rigid nature of the structure gave rise to dissatisfaction among both employees with a two-year college qualification as well as production workers.

In response to this conflict, HMI added an additional two levels to the hierarchy for production workers, extending it to six positions. Those workers with

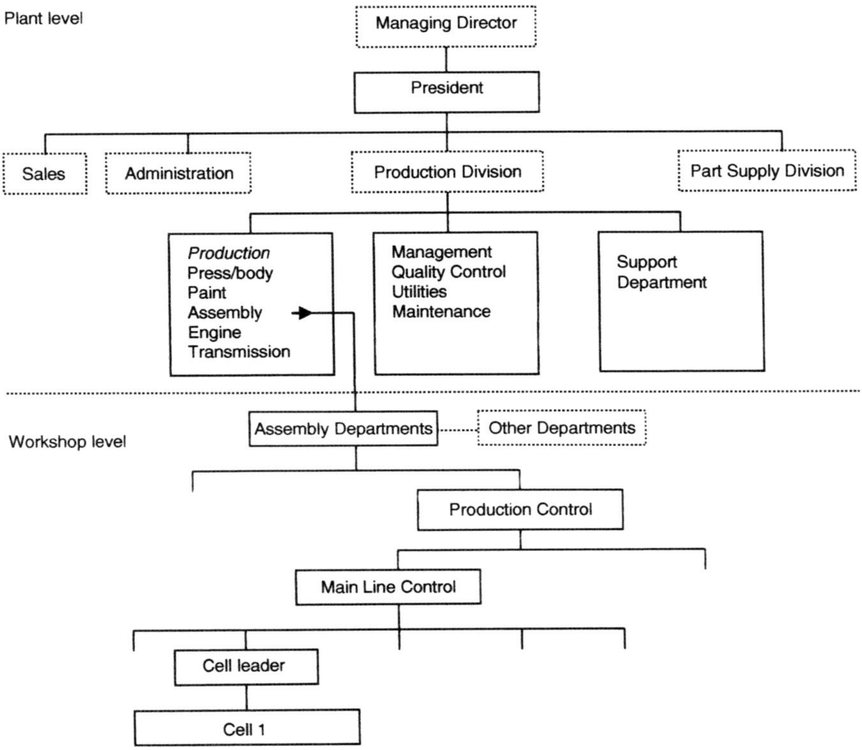

Figure 6.1 Organisational structure of production management at HMI.

Source: HMI (1999–2000c).

a two-year college qualification were therefore grouped separately from production workers in order to satisfy demands that their social status in the workplace be upgraded.

The small magnitude of these changes in the employment structure left the dual internal labour market structure largely unaffected, as promotion beyond either the supervisor or production worker ranks was not very common. Workforce discontent was therefore contained through an expansion in the number of layers within the employment structure. By restricting promotion, however, the company minimised the increase in labour costs.

This dual employment structure was also evident in HMC's internal labour market. In 2000, HMC's employment structure was organised into 18 hierarchical positions for 3 different groups – 6 management positions, 6 management assistant positions and 6 production worker positions. There was also a clear demarcation between these groups in relation to policies covering wages, promotion and welfare facilities. Similar to HMI, HMC also expanded its production employment structure from 4 positions in the early 1980s to 6 in

Table 6.1 Changes in the employment structure of HMI, 1999–2000

Position	*No. of employees*
May 1999	
Executive level	
Director	1
Senior general manager	2
General manager	2
Senior manager	7
Manager	26
Deputy manager	19
Assistant manager	55
Officer	44
Engineer	76
Manager trainee	25
General engineer trainee	64
Total no. of executive positions	321
Non executive level	
Senior assistant	27
Assistant	28
Junior assistant	20
Assistant trainee	39
Senior supervisor	3
Supervisor	106
Operative supervisor	58
Op. supervisor trainee	12
Supervisor trainee	43
Technician	172
Technician trainee	661
Cook	1
Driver	4
Workman	8
Total no. of non-executives	1,182
Total no. of employees (executive and non-executive combined)	1,503
May 2000	
Executive level	
Director	1
Senior general manager	2
General manager	3
Deputy general manager	1
Senior manager	12
Manager	27
Deputy manager	33
Assistant manager	64
Officer/Engineer	140
Manager/General engineer trainee	87
Total no. of executives	370
Junior executive level	
Junior executive-III	21
Junior executive-II	29
Junior executive-I	50
Junior executive trainee	42
Junior Engineers	
Junior engineer-III	14
Junior engineer-II	51
Junior/operative engineer-I	125
Junior engineer trainee	83
Total no. of junior executives/engineers	415
Operatives	
Technicians	230
Trainee technicians	1,210
Utility hand, attendants, workmen	95
Total no. of operatives	1,535
Total no. of employees (executive and non-executive)	2,320

Source: HMI (1999–2000a).

the 1990s to resolve discontent among its workforce. However, unlike the situation in HMI, this minor restructure of the employment hierarchy at HMC did little to abate workforce discontent. The management at HMC also placed strict limitations on the number of production workers who could advance to the highest position within the production employment structure with the majority being concentrated at the lowest levels and on the lowest wages (Kwon and O'Donnell 2001: 158–159).

A comparison of the managerial hierarchies, at the workplace level, for HMI and HMC is shown in Figure 6.2. In the case of HMI, production line workers were organised into groups of between 8 and 12 workers. This group was called a 'cell' and was supervised by a senior technician referred to as a keeper. Depending on the nature of production processes, two or three of these cells were supervised by a cell leader (or junior engineer). Although sizes varied, the structure of HMI was very similar to that which operated at HMC. At HMC the basic working group comprised between 10 and 40 workers and was guided by a supervisor who was promoted from the production workforce. Between 3 and 8 of these basic working groups came under the direct supervision of the cell leader, an assistant manager. HMC also utilised the 'keeper system', although the role of the keeper was purely to audit product quality among the production lines rather than to act as a supervisor as in the case of HMI.

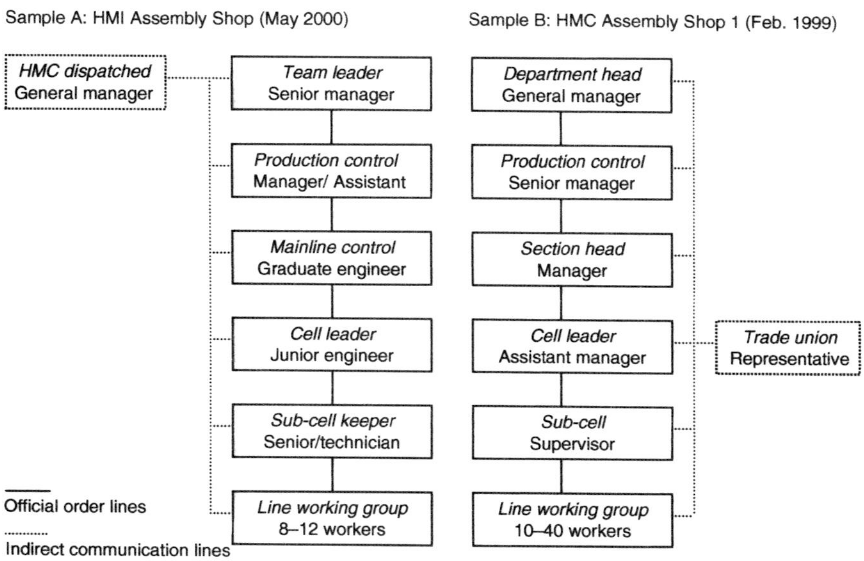

Figure 6.2 Comparison of workplace organisation and hierarchy: HMI and HMC.

Sources: HMC (1998–2001c); HMI (1999–2000c).

Expatriate management and control of the workforce

One of the most important contributing success factors of the production lines at the Chennai plant was the experience and skill of expatriate Korean HMC managers, most of who had between 15 and 20 years experience at HMC before being redeployed to HMI. These managerial employees had considerable experience in the range of production systems, from labour-intensive to increasingly mechanised and automated systems which enabled them to be highly adaptive to the difficulties and uncertainties at HMI.

Initially, Korean managers dispatched from HMC to HMI were located in all senior decision-making positions and had overall responsibility for all aspects of HMI's production operations. From early 2000, however, HMC employees were located at only two levels of HMI's employment structure: at the head of a division with responsibility for production, and at the operational level with the role of advisor to support and coordinate management activities. After 2000, further devolution of control over production operations was moved to HMI's Indian managers.

Table 6.2 shows changes in the number of HMC managers dispatched to the Chennai plant and reflects the change in the role of the Korean managers to that of a support role for local Indian management. When the plant opened, 77 HMC managers supervised approximately 1,436 Indian employees (a ratio of 1:20). In keeping with HMI's localisation policy, this ratio was increased to 1:46. The localisation of HMI management practices further enhanced the role and status of local production management personnel. HMI management thus achieved stabilisation of the internal labour market.

Issues of control in the dual structure

As noted in the previous section, HMC's Korean managers were located at two levels of HMI's production operation's hierarchy from early 2000 onwards. At the top level of the production division, an HMC-dispatched manager held responsibility for retaining control of overall production operations. An HMC manager was also responsible for the management function at the workshop level. This manager operated as an advisor in order to support and coordinate HMI's

Table 6.2 Changes in the number of HMC expatriate managers dispatched to HMI 1998–2000

Expatriate manager	*1998*	*1999*	*2000*
Total employees in HMI	1,436	1,479	2,310
Total managers dispatched from HMC	72	57	50
Ratio of managers from HMC to local employees in HMI	1:20	1:25	1:46

Source: HMI (1999–2000a).

production activities. This structure was devised as a way of overcoming the lack of local management expertise on production methods and processes. The use of HMC management however, did result in some instability in production operations during the initial phases of the plant's operation.

In addition, the Chennai plant was a greenfield site in which all production lines and equipment were fully transplanted from HMC. Employees were relocated from HMC to Chennai to ensure that HMC's production lines and related technology were fully utilised. Having HMC management at both the top level of production management and at the workshop level facilitated HMC's control over both the long-term strategic direction of HMI and daily production targets. Instead of a more traditional supervisory role, the original intention was that HMC employees would act as advisors for production operations at the workshop level. This was devised to minimise cultural conflicts between Korean and Indian employees that might have developed in the course of a more direct supervisory relationship.

All aspects of production operations, including day-to-day operations, were effectively under the direct supervision of HMC managers. Nevertheless, in order to develop local skills in production management, there was a gradual devolution of control over production to Indian managers and production workers. As this localisation process evolved, HMC's role became increasingly focused on HMI's overall production policies and operations.

Maintaining control over HMI's low-skilled workforce was central to the success of its labour-intensive product strategy and to the maintenance of quality standards. The Office of Overseas Production Technologies at HMC's Ulsan plant played a central role in controlling the production technologies and systems utilised by HMI. The office was closely involved in the planning, design and construction of overseas production facilities. Once the construction was completed, the office supported productivity and quality improvement activities and trained production specialists to operate HMC's overseas plants. The office was also involved in the development and introduction of new models for HMC's overseas plants and the application of technology into local production lines. As a result, the production processes, technologies and product models chosen by HMC's overseas plants were permitted to adjust to local circumstances, yet they still had to conform to the guidelines laid down by the Office for Overseas Production Technologies at the Ulsan plant. This effectively meant that many aspects of production systems and processes, at the Chennai plant, from construction to day-to-day operations, were effectively under the control of HMC.

At the workshop level, there were various means by which managerial employees exercised control over production line workers. Officially, senior managers were given the authority to undertake personnel assessments of their subordinates. These assessments had a significant bearing on the promotion prospects of production workers as well as their ability to access wages increases. Importance and impact of these assessments was further heightened due to the absence of trade union organisation.

Even though they were not formally represented in HMI's managerial hierarchy, HMC managers working at HMI had considerable influence over production operations. Their authority and influence was derived from being representatives of HMC as well as from their understanding and knowledge of production operations. However, HMI's localisation policy, discussed earlier, created considerable tension between local Indian managers and HMC's Korean managers. These conflicts were aggravated by misunderstandings caused by cultural differences and differences in attitudes to work.

HMI's practice of distinguishing the management hierarchy based on level of formal education and performance assessments was very similar to the approach adopted by HMC. One difference however, related to the influence of parties not formally specified in the hierarchy as control. In HMC, trade union representatives have undertaken this role in a formal capacity since 1987 and were able to exert considerable influence at the workplace level. Within HMC, trade union representatives were actively involved in operational activities such as the speed of the production line and occupational health and safety issues. Prior to the establishment of dispute resolution procedures, the involvement of trade union representatives in such matters, traditionally viewed as managerial prerogatives, caused considerable friction between management and production line workers. In HMI, where no trade union organisation existed, HMC managers had considerable informal influence over shop-floor operations.

One of the key differences between employment relations at HMI and HMC was the lack of trade union representation at HMI. At HMC's Ulsan plant, the trade union intervened to protect the industrial rights of their union members. At HMI however, despite similar structures and hierarchies, managers had an almost 'free hand' in introducing new practices.

Recruitment and selection

HMI's division of its workforce into management and production employees resulted in an internal labour market comprising executives, managerial assistants, supervisors and technician groups. As explained earlier in this chapter, formal educational qualifications were the cornerstone of recruitment decisions. A four- to six-year university degree was required for entry into executive positions, a two-year college qualification for middle management positions and high school graduation for lower levels.

The large scale of recruitment of employees at all levels over a short period resulted in tensions among Korean and Indian managerial employees, mainly due to differing backgrounds and experience. Initially, HMI claimed that it was difficult to recruit relevant and experienced managers from the Indian automobile industry mainly because of the limited development of related industries at Chennai. Hence, experienced managers from other industries were widely employed. The subsequent array of different backgrounds of senior managers created conflicts in management practices at HMI. As a result, HMI sought to recruit more senior managers from within the company.

Table 6.3 Changes in the number of recruited staff in HMI, 1997–2000

Class	*1997*	*1998*	*1999*	*May 2000*
Executive	142	150	55	24
Non-executive	209	933	742	66
Total	351	1,083	797	90

Source: HMI (1999–2000a).

Table 6.3 shows the results of HMI's recruitment of both executive and non-executive employees. Initially there was extensive recruitment for all levels of employees. Lower-level employment positions such as trainee manager, trainee supervisor and trainee technician were recruited from the local labour market.

Management sought to minimise labour costs by recruiting trainees on low wages. Once trainees were appointed, their employment contracts lasted for three years. After this time, they could be promoted to the position of technician. In the Indian labour market however, the trainee was usually regarded as a learner position in the job market with lower wages than other full-time workers. Furthermore, under Indian labour law, technicians were exempted from joining trade unions.

After making a formal application, potential production workers were given a basic written examination and then interviewed by a team of managers from human resources and production departments. In the case of management positions, potential recruits were interviewed by a team of senior managers from human resources and the respective divisions. The most important selection criteria involved an employee's personality, attitude and motivation, as well as cultural background.

The recruitment of top management positions were undertaken by HMC's head office in Korea, while recruitment of lower-level positions was undertaken by HMI management in India.

Training and education

HMI developed a range of training and education programmes for different groups of employees. Table 6.4 gives an overview of these training programmes, their frequency and the employees to which they are targeted.

In total, 64 training programmes were instituted for various employment categories at HMI. The basic orientation programme, a two-day workshop, was designed to induct newly recruited employees into HMI. It provided a general background to HMI and included a tour of production operations.

Other training programmes were more job specific. The major objective of the executive and management development programmes was to enhance the managerial capacity of senior and middle managers by developing their ability to

Table 6.4 Training and education programmes at HMI

Programme	*No. of programmes*	*Target employees*
Basic orientation training	49	Grade-level training
Executive development programme	2	Executive positions
Management development programme	8	Management positions
Staff development programme	2	Management assistant positions
Supervisor development programme	1	Supervisor positions
Workmen development programme	2	Technician positions
Total	64	

Source: HMI (1999-2000a).

think strategically, focus on improving work methods and quality, and to provide training in the strategic significance of their functional area to the organisation. The staff development programme was used to improve the roles of clerical staff in supporting executives and managers through the provision of efficient documentation and improved time management. The supervisor development programme aimed to enhance leadership skills within the workplace and explored a range of techniques for improving workplace productivity. The production worker development programme aimed to motivate production workers to actively participate in workplace productivity improvement campaigns through employee suggestion schemes and quality control systems.

A central focus of training was the moulding of employee's attitudes to fit with HMI's corporate culture. Knowledge of Hyundai's cultural and corporate values, as well as communication skills, comprised 4 of the 16 hours of basic orientation training. Cultural values such as proactive working attitudes, effective interpersonal skills and perceiving the company as a family community were key components of other training programmes. Cultural values were emphasised in order to promote workforce loyalty and to minimise internal conflicts between the various employment groups and between these groups and HMC managers. Efforts to maximise workforce harmony were also undertaken to minimise tensions between the workers from different levels within the traditional Indian caste hierarchy. The Indian caste system is traditionally organised into four castes. Within HMI, some 28 per cent of the workforce came from the upper caste, 52 per cent from the middle castes and 20 per cent from the lowest caste. This caste composition has been reflected in the employment structure of HMI.

Newly recruited production workers were given a two-day basic orientation training and then allocated to a specific production department. Most of their initial job training was carried out on the production line. It took a further two weeks to familiarise themselves with the immediate cycle of production tasks. This was followed by a job rotation programme that exposed production workers to the skills required on other production lines. This multi-skilling programme was possible within this timeframe because of the detailed division of labour on the production lines where jobs were highly fragmented into relatively simple and repetitive cycles of tasks for low-skilled workers.

Wages

The wage policy was a most critical factor in HMI's production operation. Increases in both wages and production costs affected HMI's market position. Nevertheless, HMI was able to improve labour productivity and retain its skilled workforce. In the absence of trade unions and collective bargaining, company-initiated wage rises were the only source of increased income for production workers. Within this context, HMI management developed a range of wage policies to achieve its basic goals of minimising labour costs while developing a skilled workforce and avoiding industrial conflicts and retaining its skilled workforce.

The wage levels of HMI employees increased annually via increments normally paid in April each year. The validity of the wage structure was tested by three annual reviews to ensure that it was in line with changes in the employment structure and the external labour market. Table 6.5 outlines the salary structure for production workers of HMI which is comprised of a basic wage and various allowances. Rather than a fixed wage, HMI provided a range of welfare allowances which took into account such items as the cost of living, housing rentals and children's education expenses. There was considerable variation between the ratio of the basic wage to allowances depending on where the employee was placed in the employment hierarchy. For example, most managerial employee's total wages comprised at least 60 per cent paid as a basic wage. This figure for production workers was usually around 30 per cent or less of their overall remuneration.

Furthermore, as seen in Table 6.5, the ratio of basic wage to allowances declined the lower the employee was on the production worker employment structure declining from 36 per cent basic wage for senior technicians to 24 per cent for trainee positions.

Table 6.5 Salary structure for technicians employed by HMI (in %)

Grade	*Basic wage*	*CL*	*HRA*	*Flex. all*	*Others*	*Total (%)*
Senior technician A	35.8	21.6	12.9	12.5	17.2	100
Supervisor 1	34.5	22.6	13.5	12.3	17.1	100
Technician B	32.8	19.4	11.6	19.4	16.8	100
Trainee 1	24.0	26.6	12.0	18.9	18.5	100

Source: HMI (1999–2000a).

Notes
The index was based on actual amount of the salary; CL = cost of living allowance; HRA = housing rent allowance; Flex. all = flexible allowance; Others include conveyance allowance, leave travel allowance, children education allowance, provident fund and so on.

Table 6.6 shows the changes in differentials in the wages between executive and non-executive employment positions since 1999. While a wide gap between executive and non-executive positions was maintained, it was slightly reduced from 6 times more than production workers in June 1999 to 5.6 times by May 2000.

HMI increased the monthly wages for production workers from 3,990 rupees in June 1999 to 4,600 rupees in May 2000. This was associated with HMI's rapid growth in market share and its increased capacity to absorb increases in labour costs. Over the course of 2000–2001, HMI revised its wages policy for production workers in line with growing workforce discontent with low basic wages. However, HMI was still able to retain its competitive position when compared against the wages paid by other automobile companies. According to information supplied by other auto companies, HMI was at the lower end of the foreign-owned enterprises, in terms of wage costs, but was higher than most locally owned firms (see Table 6.7).

One of the key contributors to sustaining low labour costs was the concentration of a large proportion of the workforce in the trainee category, on three-year contracts. Yet, this policy was a significant source of workforce discontent. In response to pressure for wage increases, HMI management increased the wages of production workers. As shown in Table 6.7, there was a sharp increase in the wages of both junior technicians and trainees during early 2000. These improvements in the wages of junior staff reduced wage dissatisfaction as HMI compared favourably with other employers in the industry. For example, HMI's trainee 1 group received 2,400 rupees per month while those in Ashok-Leland and Maruti received only 1,000 and 1,500 rupees. Despite these wage increases, by maintaining the largest component of HMI's workforce in trainee groups HMI has been able to control its overall labour costs and retain its competitive position in the automobile market. Hence, despite providing wage increases for junior staff, HMI was able to utilise its internal labour market structure to keep a large proportion of staff at the lowest levels of the structure and maintain control of its overall cost structure.

Promotion

Control over promotion through the internal labour market structure was the principal means by which HMI management maintained low labour costs and improved labour productivity. It provided employees with access to an annual wage increment. A promotion round occurred every April and involved two committees – one for executive positions that was overseen by divisional heads and the head of human resources and one for non-executive employees overseen by divisional managers and the human resources division.

HMI required employees to serve a minimum number of years before they became eligible for promotion. This system was designed so that it would take over 20 years for a management trainee to become a general manager, 11 years for a junior engineer or executive trainee to rise to grade III and 23 years for a production worker to become a senior technician B. However, despite the fixed years of service required for promotion, some flexibility was applied to manage

Table 6.6 Monthly change in labour costs at HMI by type of employment position: 1999–2000

	Month											
	06/99	*07/99*	*08/99*	*09/99*	*10/99*	*11/99*	*12/99*	*01/00*	*02/00*	*03/00*	*04/00*	*05/00*
Executive groups												
Nos. (A)	328	334	341	348	349	353	350	351	352	357	371	370
Total (B)	7,686	7,768	9,528	8,025	11,329	7,251	8,122	8,447	8,185	8,312	9,512	9,557
B/A	23.4	23.2	27.9	23.1	32.5	20.5	23.2	24.1	23.3	23.3	25.6	25.8
Non-executive groups												
Nos. (A)	1,379	1,615	1,853	1,862	1,865	1,879	1,885	1,903	1,924	1,939	1,940	1,953
Total (B)	5,361	5,817	6,870	6,535	11,046	7,159	6,927	7,199	7,187	7,170	8,764	8,951
B/A	3.9	3.6	3.7	3.5	5.9	3.8	3.7	3.8	3.7	3.7	4.5	4.6

Sources: HMI (1999–2000a).

Note
Nos. = number of employees; sudden increase in total labour cost in Oct. 1999 was largely attributed to the incentive of HMI given to employees; Amount: 1,000 rupees.

Table 6.7 Changes in monthly salary of HMI for technician groups by comparison with other local companies

	HMI			*Ashok-Leland*	*Hindustan Motors*	*Lucas-TVS*	*Daewoo*	*Maruti*
	March 2000	*April 2000*	*% increase*					
Senior T.	8,666	10,366	19.3	8,461	N/A	8,405	9,206	13,148
Technician B	64,441	8,223	27.7	8,051	10,169	8,365	5,404	11,192
Technician A	5,712	7,754	35.7	7,390	9,962	8,347	5,252	10,393
Junior T.2	5,006	7,144	42.7	N/A	9,730	8,297	4,789	N/A
Junior T.1	4,070	7,098	74.4	N/A	N/A	N/A	N/A	N/A
Trainee 3	2,500	3,000	20.0	N/A	N/A	1,675	N/A	1,500
Trainee 2	2,250	2,700	20.0	1,200	N/A	1,475	N/A	1,500
Trainee 1	2,000	2,400	20.0	1,000	N/A	1,300	N/A	1,500

Source: HMI (1999–2000a).

Note
T. = Technician; Amount: rupees; the amount is based on the average of the salary; samples of the salary of other companies are from early 2000.

bottlenecks within the employment structure and to promote exceptional employees with distinguished performance records.

The promotion policy was effective in minimising increases in labour costs. A large proportion of production employees were located in the trainee groups and it was anticipated that many of these workers would move to another company after three years in search of improvements in wages and conditions. Such labour turnover facilitated HMI's efforts to restrict promotion opportunities and control overall labour costs. Table 6.8 shows the number and percentage of workers who were promoted in 1999 and 2000. The figure shows that as employees began to acquire an increasing number of years of service they began to move through the employment structure. A greater proportion of managerial employees were promoted compared with production workers.

A key tool for determining promotion in HMI was the performance appraisal system. There were four types of appraisal systems in place – two for executive staff, one for non-executive employees and one for trainees. The appraisal process occurred at the end of a one-year cycle when employees were reviewed by three assessors: the rater, the reviewer and by a manager overseeing the entire process. Initial performance assessments were undertaken by the manager in charge of the section, department or division of the production line. For example, a production trainee was initially assessed by their production supervisor (rater) and this rating was reviewed by the sectional head and then screened by the departmental head (overseer). Table 6.9 outlines the assessment criteria. Employees were rated on a four-point scale of outstanding, good, fair and unsatisfactory. Assessments affected promotion opportunities and the extent of the wage increases. As promotion opportunities for production workers were deliberately contained, the appraisal system yielded very modest wage increases.

The performance appraisal system enhanced managerial control as it intensified competition among production workers to achieve the highest performance ratings. Social and cultural variables were also important in determining the overall performance assessment. These included behavioural criteria such as discipline, working attitude, team cooperation, punctuality and attendance. Such assessments were inherently subjective and there were frequent internal conflicts between management and production workers over the ratings. The HMI appraisal system was similar to that used by HMC.

Table 6.8 Promotion of employees at HMI: 1999 and 2000

Number of employees	*1999*		*2000*	
	Nos. promoted	*% of total workforce*	*Nos. promoted*	*% of total workforce*
Executive	24	10	56	21.7
Non-executive	39	10	57	12.7
Total	63	10	113	16.0

Source: HMI (1999–2000a).

Table 6.9 HMI appraisal criteria for executive and non-executive groups

Executive groups	*Non-executive groups*
Work output	Work output
Quality at work	Quality at work
Cost consciousness	Cost consciousness
Job knowledge	Job knowledge
Ability for self-development	Interpersonal competence
Interpersonal competence	Communication
Communication	Punctuality and attendance
Creativity	Team Cooperation
Attitude	Attitude
	Discipline

Source: HMI (1999–2000a).

Industrial conflict at HMI

Traditionally, the trade union movement in India has been closely associated with left-wing parties in Indian politics (Bhattacherjee 2001). A range of labour standards and rights for industrial workers have been secured by both political agitation and legal reforms. For example, the *Indian Industrial Relations Act* secures workers' rights for freedom of association and allows multi-unionism within and across workplaces, although workers may be affiliated with only one union. The Act also permits third-party intervention by trade union organisations in resolving industrial issues for their members at the workplace (Venkata Ratnam 1995).

Since the large-scale industrial strikes of the early and mid-1980s, which coincided with political unrest, the degree of industrial conflict in India has stabilised. Industrial conflicts in the northern part of India have generally been more intense than in the south. This is because of the major concentration of industrial estates and political activism in Northern India. In 2000, trade unions were organised in 24 of the 28 major car manufacturers in the Indian automobile industry. Multiple trade unions were represented in six companies while the others were single union workplaces. However, there were no trade unions in four foreign-owned or joint venture companies that included Ford, Volvo, Toyota and HMI. There were two major industrial strikes in the automobile industry in the late 1990s. The first was organised by the Ascot-Faridabad Trade Union in November 1998 and was triggered by a dispute over compensation and wages. The strike lasted for 70 days. The second dispute was by the Hindustan Trade Union in July 1999 to improve factory conditions and increase production workers wages, and involved a 30-days work stoppage.

Since the inception of HMI, trade unions have been unsuccessful in their attempts to organise the workers at the Chennai plant. During the expansion of production operations at Chennai from 1997 to 1999, there were no major industrial disputes or successful union organising efforts. However, as production stabilised and HMI's market share and profitability grew from late 1999, there were several attempts to unionise the workplace both from within the plant as well as through external union activities. Some unions attempted to recruit HMI workers during the period before the government elections in Chennai in 2001.

Some senior production workers began to express dissatisfaction in a more overt manner with HMI's management practices. In early 1999, there were several fragmented industrial disputes by workers employed by joint local vendors of HMI, including Donghee, Pyunghwa, Hwasung and Samrib. The issues in dispute concerned lack of job security, wage increases and welfare improvements. The disputes had an adverse effect on HMI's production efficiency as these suppliers had a monopoly of the supply of critical production parts to HMI. These disputes were eventually resolved by the intervention of HMI management.

There were various internal sources of industrial conflict at HMI. Disputes arose because of a lack of appropriate grievance procedures to effectively channel industrial discontent among the workforce. During the early period of the plant's operation, HMI management were focused on production issues. Institutional mechanisms for resolving workplace disputes were given a lesser priority, particularly as there were few overt conflicts or collective actions by workers. Over the years, however, concerns over work intensification and low wages became an increasing focus for collective workforce discontent. Production workers were resentful that their wage increases were restrained by management and that they had limited access to promotions.

Another source of industrial conflict arose from differences between the local Indian managers and the Korean managers dispatched to Chennai by HMC. There were conflicts over decision-making when local managers were placed under the direct supervision of Korean managers. Although these dispatched managers subsequently became advisors or coordinators, there were conflicts with Indian managers due to the differences in the management styles of the two groups.

These intra-management conflicts were further complicated when combined with the conflicts that occurred between Indian caste groups. HMI's workforce comprised 28 per cent from the upper caste, 52 per cent from the middle caste and 20 per cent from the lowest caste. The caste composition of the HMI workforce was also an issue for trade unions, who were generally aligned with communist or socialist parties and were unsympathetic to grievances based on caste.

HMI management preferred to exclude unions from the workplace. This was a key factor in HMC's decision to invest in a production facility at Chennai in preference to the Northern part of India. As mentioned earlier, workers and trade unions in the southern part of India were traditionally more compliant than their northern counterparts. However, HMI management encouraged the formation of a works committee which would encourage workforce commitment to HMI. This policy had its origins in experiences within Korea where HMC's overtly hostile approach to trade unionism and the resultant industrial unrest resulted in a substantial increase in HMC's cost structure. This constrained the growth of the company in Korea from the mid-1980s to the early 1990s. However, in the mid-1990s, HMC changed its approach to one of accepting the existence of an enterprise trade union in Korea. Its industrial relations strategy thereafter focused on trying to ensure that the union's goals were moderate.

Beginning in 2000, HMI management began to introduce policies to address workforce discontent through an institutionalised form of conflict resolution. In April 2000, a Works Committee was introduced which comprised membership from management and production workers. Table 6.10 shows the composition of the Works Committee. Workers were asked to sign an agreement that they would fulfil the requirements of their employment contract, which was ratified by the relevant government agency.

The Works Committee met monthly to resolve disagreements over issues such as wages, employment conditions and the pace of the production line. The Committee was also used by management to monitor a range of industrial matters and develop solutions to workforce grievances before they became serious. The Committee was also a forum in which management could disseminate its policies to production workers. As a result of the operation of the Workshop Committee, there were significant increases in wages for junior-level workers (25 per cent) and regular production workers (30 per cent) in May 2000. However, one of the key problems in the operation of the Works Committee, from the worker's perspective, was the prohibition on it organising strikes. Hence, in place of an independent trade union organisation, management implemented a more limited consultation system. This meant that if there were unresolved conflicts, there were a few methods available to assist with their resolution. HMI management also introduced other committees such as the plant committee, welfare committee, safety committee and canteen committee to deal with a range of employee concerns, although these were also criticised for their limited powers of action.

In response to complaints from production workers about its employment relations policies, HMI management revised its practices to promote greater loyalty to the company and a more cooperative approach from the production workforce. Furthermore, in the process of recruiting production workers, HMI screened applicants for likely membership or previous membership of a trade union. Junior executives were also banned from joining a trade union. These actions reduced the overall pool of potential members available to Indian trade unions to organise.

Table 6.10 Composition of membership of the Works Committee at HMI

Management	*Production workers*
President	
General manager – Human Resources Division	Three production workers (signed in standing order)
General manager – Human Resources Division (HMC)	One from the press/body shop
Deputy general manager – Human Resources Division	One from the assembly shop
General manager – Production Division	One from the engine transmission shop
Deputy general manager – assembly shop	

Sources: HMI (1999–2000a); HMI (1999–2000b).

HMI management also enhanced its cultural education programmes to promote family activities and to disseminate propaganda regarding the disruptive potential of the union movement. During 2000, for example, more than 4,000 family members of HMI employees were invited to participate in factory tours and other family events. Improving welfare facilities was another important element in HMI's strategy to improve employment relations. HMI management introduced loan system for employees to cover the cost of marriage, children's education and medical services. Recreation facilities were also provided for workers and their families.

HMI intensified its efforts within the production facilities to further restrict the development of trade unions. After the industrial disputes among their vendors, HMI management intervened to review their vendor's production management practices and attempted to minimise the potential for further industrial unrest.

HMI management established close relationships with various industrial relations agencies such as employer associations, government bodies, car manufactures and other interest groups in the region. HMI increased its recruitment from local communities in which its production operations were located. HMI also supported various local community activities such as medical and recreation facilities, education programmes and libraries. All these community activities contributed to the development of a more favourable corporate image for HMI at the local level.

Comparing employment relations at HMI and HMC

Overall, the basic elements of employment relations practices applied by HMI were similar to those used by HMC in Korea. The application of these practices was easier in a greenfield site with a new workforce than in more traditional industrial regions of India. All the production technologies and processes used in HMI also originated from HMC. Management sought to link particular employment relations practices to HMI's production processes.

HMI used a similar approach to managing its employees as HMC did in Korea. Both applied a dual approach to the development of internal labour markets that divided the workforce into two different groups, managerial employees and production workers, by using different ports of entry into the internal labour market, based on different educational qualifications. Clear demarcations existed in the hierarchies of both HMI and HMC between production workers and management assistant positions. Furthermore, different employment relations policies on issues such as wages, promotion and welfare facilities were applied to each group. HMC also expanded its production employment structure over the years from four in the early 1980s and six in the 1990s to resolve discontent among the production workforce. However, the restructuring by HMC was largely undertaken in an *ad hoc* manner and served to restrict the numbers of production workers who could be promoted to the highest levels of the production employment structure (Kwon and O'Donnell 2001: 158–159).

In relation to resolving industrial conflicts, HMI practices were very similar to those of HMC in Korea. From the mid-1980s and the advent of militant independent unions at HMC, management have struggled to develop policies and tactics to minimise industrial conflicts in their workplaces. Industrial unrest at HMC has become a national parameter each year for industrial relations in other sectors in Korea. All major interest groups such as government, the Korean Confederation of Trade Unions and other employers associations, intervened in order to reduce industrial disputes at HMC, over the last 15 years. As a result, HMC has adopted a more sophisticated approach to dealing with trade unions in recent times.

Nevertheless, there were some important differences between employment relations practices adopted by HMI in Chennai and HMC in Korea. HMI management found it difficult to fully implement performance-based employment practices at Chennai. Indian employees preferred to have a similar approach to reward management for each employment group. This is a reflection of their social background in caste structure, with employees in each caste having comparably similar rewards across the caste. Indian managers also tended to be very concerned to maintain differences based on personal status and social position. This created difficulties when they conflicted with the supervisory role of the dispatched managers from HMC. In response to these intra-managerial tensions, some employment relations and production management practices at HMI were changed to meet the concerns of Indian managers. HMI developed a larger number of hierarchical positions within its employment structure than was evident at HMC in Korea. HMI management found it difficult to develop formalised or institutionalised communication channels, especially across different employment groups because of demarcations between social classes and castes and a preference for using informal networks in communication. Therefore, in contrast to HMC in Korea, HMI management had to develop both formal and informal communication channels with their employees.

7 Conclusion

Global and local?

What lessons can be learned from the experience of Hyundai Motor Company (HMC) in India? To what degree has HMC transferred its production systems and employment relations policies from Korea to India? Is there something unique about the way in which Hyundai Motors India (HMI) has managed Foreign Direct Investment (FDI), production systems and employment relations at the Chennai plant? How does the experience of Hyundai in India compare with its previous failure in Canada? Does HMI represent a turning point in HMC's globalisation strategy?

These questions and others have been asked throughout the preceding chapters of this book. This concluding chapter reflects on some of the insights gained into a relatively new area of scholarship and extends the analysis to consider the future challenges facing HMI and other Korean companies as they seek to produce beyond their own country's boundaries.

Globalisation and the world auto industry

HMC is part of an increasingly global automobile industry. The US carmakers, particularly Ford, and carmakers in Europe, led the way in the 1960s, the Japanese ascended in the 1980s and the 1990s witnessed the development of strategic alliances which came to dominate world output. In the early twenty-first century, the industry faces overcapacity and stagnating demand in existing markets which has resulted in fierce competition to capture emerging markets. However, instead of a world vehicle market or 'world car', it seems that regional rather than global strategies may offer more opportunities for automobile manufacturers.

This growth in international trade has been facilitated by the development of new production systems. During the 1950s, American manufacturers became major players due to their ability to maximise economies of scale through a mass production system. Their successes led to Fordism becoming highly influential worldwide. By the 1980s, however, Toyota and other Japanese auto manufacturers had developed a superior system known as flexible specialisation or lean production, which allowed the Japanese to overcome the restraints and limitations of mass production. Despite its weaknesses, lean production was widely adopted and has become part of many production systems in the industry today.

Although there are some significant differences between markets and firms which prevent the auto industry's convergence towards a single paradigm of production, some global networks have developed. The term 'techno-globalization' is used to describe the way in which automotive companies have created global technology networks and technical alliances, in areas such as research and development in order to reduce costs and remain competitive, especially in response to the emergence of producers in the newly industrialising economies such as China, India and South America. Global partnerships between suppliers, assemblers, equipment producers, dealers and clients have also developed. It is evident that auto companies are assuming more of a management and coordination role as service providers by outsourcing production, components and labour in a multi-tiered system of newly industrialising economies and developed market economies. In this way, automobile production has become increasingly complex but the benefits of these new approaches have yet to be fully realised.

Globalization and FDI in the Korean auto industry

The Korean auto industry expanded rapidly during the 1970s and 1980s with the assistance of investment and export strategies which were designed to facilitate the country's rapid industrialisation. Until the late 1990s, the Korean government discouraged inward FDI and used loans to finance investment. Like the Japanese, the Koreans utilised purchased technology and reverse engineering rather than forming technical alliances beyond their borders. However, the *chaebols*' reliance on large loans from the state-controlled banking sector to finance debt- and volume-based growth strategies significantly contributed to the Asian financial crisis of the late 1990s. The crisis arose from unsustainable debt levels and the Korean government no longer agreed to act as an agent for loans. The Korean auto industry underwent major restructuring and companies were forced to revise their expansionary strategies in order to focus more on efficiency and profitability rather than increasing concerns about market share and company size. In some cases, such as the Hyundai group, this also meant restructuring the *chaebols* in order to reconstitute their businesses into more viable entities.

Exporting has been an important part of Korea's industrialisation strategy for Korea and has meant that the auto companies, like many large Korean firms, have adopted a more international outlook. The automobile industry originated in response to government plans for the development of local manufacturing for the domestic market. This soon led to the development of Korean export models utilising a mass production system. The achievements of Korean auto companies in the domestic market laid the foundation for aggressive expansion into the international market and led the way to globalisation. Indeed, the scale of investment being undertaken meant that companies needed to export in order to avoid excess capacity in the domestic market. The Koreans adopted the Japanese entry strategy of using price competition to enter at the low end of the market and gradually move upwards as their market share and competitiveness increased.

Prior to 1985, Korean automobile exports were primarily directed to the EC but, as the 1980s progressed, the United States became a major export destination. By the second half of the 1990s, Korean export destinations had diversified to include newly industrialising countries in Asia and South America.

Korean auto companies have thus experienced a gradual progression towards global production. Subsidiaries in industrialised market economies have mostly been representative offices and sales companies but strategic alliances have been established to improve technical capabilities. By contrast, agreements with newly industrialising economies have focused on assembly plants and sales companies. In this way, the globalisation and investment strategies of Korean auto companies have tended to be market oriented rather than being based on a country or region's geographical proximity to Korea. The four stages of global production can therefore be summarised as direct exportation through independent sales agents in host countries, followed by the establishment of their own sales offices, the introduction of knock-down assembly through joint ventures with local partners in less developed countries and eventually complete overseas production systems. The Korean auto industry is yet to develop an extensive global supply chain and, as will be discussed in the following pages in relation to HMC, it will need to continue to build upon recent advancements in overseas production and coordination of production, marketing and technology development to achieve a mature global production system.

The emergence of HMC as a global auto manufacturer

Within the context of the Korean automobile industry's globalisation, HMC has become the nation's leading auto manufacturer. Early partnerships with Ford and Mitsubishi eventually led to HMC's first original model, the *Pony*, in 1976. Following the *Pony's* success, HMC rapidly expanded its production capacity and established plants in Canada, Turkey, India, China and Malaysia. Despite setbacks following the Asian financial crisis in the late 1990s and the failure of its plant in Canada, HMC has emerged as Korea's strongest automobile company and has achieved its goal of becoming one of the top ten auto manufacturers in the world. The particular success of HMI in India symbolises a turning point as HMC further expands its international production, including in the United States.

HMC's production strategy has been instrumental to its emergence as a global automobile company. HMC's early alliance with Ford led to the development of a Fordist assembly line and, following the success of the *Pony*, a large mechanised mass production system. Mitsubishi was also influential in providing technological support and training, production equipment and machinery. Since the mid-1980s, production has intensified as a result of automation and mechanisation.

The success of HMC's manufacturing strategy has been closely linked to its employment relations policies and practices. It was not until the mid-1970s that the growing mass production workforce necessitated the formalisation of HMC's previously *ad hoc* approach to employment relations. The Korean government's prohibition on many trade union activities prior to 1987 allowed management to unilaterally determine the wages and conditions of employees. Employers thereby achieved massive increases in production by imposing low wages and work intensification. HMC was initially aggressive and hostile towards unions but a series of labour law reforms after 1987 forced HMC to engage in collective bargaining. The success of union campaigns to achieve wage increases and the implementation of new welfare measures undermined the previous bases of HMC's competitiveness, which were low labour costs and work intensification. HMC had to meet the challenge of maintaining its competitiveness with a unionised workforce.

Although there have been some setbacks, HMC has been successful both within Korea as well as in its export markets. In the past decade, HMC has established plants overseas as part of its globalisation strategy. In cooperation with Mitsubishi, HMC's first venture was an assembly plant in Quebec, Canada, which opened in 1985. This operation was unsuccessful and the plant was closed in 1993. Although the plant's closure was primarily due to disappointing sales, another contributing factor was HMC's failure to successfully manage employment relations. In 1996, HMC relaunched its globalisation strategy by establishing a wholly owned subsidiary company in India, known as HMI.

Production systems in HMI

HMI's success has rested on a combination of its production systems, employment relations and investment. HMI's key strategy was to produce high-quality vehicles at a lower cost than its rivals. To achieve this goal, its policies and production systems closely resembled those of HMC's Ulsan plant in Korea. Over time, HMI has tailored its approach to meet the demands of the Indian labour force, components suppliers and consumers. The main difference from HMC is that HMI's semi-mechanised production systems are more labour intensive than the highly automated systems at the Ulsan plant. Lower labour costs associated with the comparatively low-paid and less-skilled Indian workforce have minimised the need to introduce mechanised and automated production systems and thereby enabled HMI to contain its production costs. HMI sought to maximise this labour-intensive system by applying the principles of 'scientific management' to simplify production tasks. This also made it easier for HMI to replace and train unskilled production workers on the assembly line in a short period of time. Nevertheless, a job rotation system for technicians was utilised to offset monotony and fatigue and to foster multi-skilling and productivity. HMI sought to maintain quality standards through its Quality Development Department and job suggestion scheme.

HMI has retained close ties to HMC in the areas of research and development and the management of the supply chain. Korean suppliers initially provided the majority of parts for HMI in order to ensure high levels of quality. A process of sourcing parts from local suppliers was introduced but encountered problems associated with the geographical separation of suppliers in the north from HMI in Southern India, plus poor quality control and delays which led to production stoppages. However, HMI's efforts to improve the reliability and efficiency of its supply chain eventually succeeded in significantly reducing production stoppages by 2000.

The management of employment relations in HMI

Due to the labour-intensive nature of HMI's production systems, the success of the company has also been closely related to its employment relations. Initially, Korean managers dominated HMI and their experience and skill in automobile production were crucial to HMI's early success. Whilst their leadership assisted in overcoming the initial lack of local management expertise, it also created some tension with local managers and workers. As the localisation policy was implemented, HMI took greater responsibility for the production policies and overall operations. Nevertheless, HMC retained considerable control through its Office of Overseas Production Technologies which monitored the Chennai plant.

Entry to jobs within HMI has been based on formal educational qualifications. Employees received a basic wage plus various allowances. Wage policies sought to contain annual increases as much as possible whilst developing and retaining a skilled workforce. Although HMI was forced to revise its policies in response to workforce discontent with low basic wages, it succeeded in containing labour costs and maintaining its market competitiveness by keeping a high concentration of the workforce in trainee positions and restricting their promotion to higher ranks within the company.

The absence of trade unions at HMI has made it difficult for workers to air and resolve their grievances. HMI established a Works Committee and revised employment relations policies and training programmes to promote employee loyalty and cooperation. HMI also screened out potential labour and trade union activists through a careful recruitment and selection process. Cultural education programmes were used to encourage family values and limit the appeal of unions, HMI-supported various community programmes to enhance its corporate image. In addition, links were made with components suppliers and industrial agencies to help minimise industrial unrest. Through these means HMI sought to develop workplace harmony and reduce conflict. However, HMI may need to consider the possibility that unions may establish a presence at the Chennai plant in the future and the company may be required to engage in collective bargaining with unions.

Future challenges

The case study shows that HMI has used a combination of production and employment relations strategies at its Chennai plant. The company successfully used a semi-mechanised, labour-intensive production system to enter the Indian market with a medium-priced model and rapidly increased its market share. It has differentiated its production system from HMC through its focus on labour-intensive production in order to utilise its relatively cheap, non-unionised workforce. Whilst HMC adopted a similar approach during its early stages of operation in Korea, its production system has since become highly automated and mechanised. The introduction of a management system which simplifies production tasks and creates high divisions of labour has also made it easier to replace and train unskilled production workers on the assembly line in a relatively short period of time. Hence, in some ways, HMI has learnt from the Canadian experience by controlling labour and also by producing automobiles which are appropriate for the Indian market. HMI's firm control over its workforce has also enabled it, thus far, to avoid the discord experienced in Canada where the workers, although non-unionised, were willing to challenge management decisions and policies. These circumstances prevented the full implementation of HMC's employment relations policies in Canada.

Despite these advantages, HMI will need to upgrade its production system and reassess its employment relations policies if it seeks to build on its market share in India. Its semi-mechanised, labour-intensive mass production system has served its initial purpose as a low-cost, competitive entry strategy. However, as discussed in Chapter 1, the global trend is away from traditional mass production towards the high-quality system of lean production, or at least some hybrid form of it. This suggests that HMI must adapt and change or risk its losing long-term competitiveness. Meeting this challenge, however, will require increased FDI to finance the upgrading of technology and production systems to reach the required level of sophistication. Technical alliances will need to be more vigorously pursued to facilitate the shift towards more automated and mechanised production. More significantly, it will require the recruitment and training of more highly skilled and highly paid workers and an appropriate system of labour–management relations.

Employment relations is a very critical issue for HMI in the immediate and longer-term future. The control HMI has enjoyed over its employees has allowed it to successfully minimise its labour costs and thereby maximise the efficiencies arising from its labour-intensive operations. By contrast to the Hyundai plants in Korea and Canada, managerial control has been facilitated by South India's more favourable environment for employment relations as a non-unionised greenfield site. However, this situation is changing. The number of Korean managers from HMC located at the Chennai plant is being reduced and less-experienced Indian managers are having to assume greater responsibilities. There appears to be growing discontent with management policies and decisions as well as with wages and conditions. It would appear that HMC's experiences in Korea and Canada may have influenced HMI's reluctance to recognise unions and engage in collective bargaining. However, the methods of close supervision, strict demarcation between production workers and management, and restricted wage increases and promotion may be difficult to achieve in the future. HMI has placed strong emphasis on employee identification with the company in its training programmes and has successfully prevented employees from unionising. However, if this approach is to succeed in the longer term, HMI may need to grant employees greater opportunities to be involved in its decision-making processes and to have representation through unions or other means, such as enterprise-based unions or work councils.

HMI has achieved initial success in the Indian market. However, in order that HMI builds upon its early success it will need to forge a new approach. This will need to take into account the circumstances of India and to facilitate the development of a more sophisticated, high-quality, high-volume production system. Such a production system will place considerable pressure on employment relations which have been based on maximising the advantages of low-cost labour.

HMC faced a similar situation in the period following 1987 when it could no longer rely on low labour costs to minimise its production costs. However, as unions gained power and were successful in achieving wage increases and implementing an extensive welfare system, the foundations of HMC's competitiveness were undermined and the company had to adopt new strategies such as moving production overseas.

As HMC becomes a leading global automobile manufacturer, a much greater proportion of its production will be undertaken outside Korea. HMC will need to embrace the global trend of large auto companies of fostering global supply chains and coordinating production, marketing and technology. The success of HMI has encouraged HMC to continue expanding production to other countries. Yet, HMI's initial advantages of low-cost labour are quickly fading. In addition to production and technology improvements, the experiences of Hyundai in Canada and India suggest that employment relations must combine core company policies with the unique needs and practices of the local environment in which the company is operating. For example, in India, HMI has had to institute a more hierarchical organisational structure to reflect local industry practices, culture and customs, especially the caste system. This highlights the fact that there are complex interactions between pressures of convergence or uniformity at the global level while there are also divergent tendencies at the local level.

In the future, HMC must learn to adapt its new production systems and technologies to the local market and employment relations. HMC's global ambitions will be constrained unless it learns to stay abreast of international trends whilst also meeting the unique needs and circumstances of the local workers, industry partners and consumers of its various operations and markets around the world. HMC's long-term success and sustainability will depend upon the company's ability to evolve and meet these challenges.

It should be noted that HMC is pursuing a different strategy in the United States. In 2005, HMC opened a new plant in Alabama which utilised a highly advanced automated system with a capacity of producing 120,000 vehicles per annum. HMC is also expanding its joint venture operations in China and seeking to move to the medium end of the Chinese market.

Afterword

One key contribution provided by this volume is solid evidence that the work practices adopted by the HMC at their auto assembly plants in India and Canada have comprised a mixture of company-specific practices and adaptations to local conditions and local institutional pressures and constraints. This evidence is consistent with other research on auto and other industry 'transplants' that have been built in a variety of countries, including the United States, by Japanese, Hyundai and other 'foreign'-based multi-national corporations (MNCs). Instead of the standardised application of corporate practice, the research reveals a process of hybridisation and adaptation, with considerable variety in the terms and extent of hybridisation across plants, companies and countries.

The fact that Hyundai is not spreading a consistent 'Hyundai way' across plants as it expands globally adds further evidence that there is not a simple convergence occurring in the global auto industry to one set of practices. The lack of global convergence is even more apparent in the fact that Hyundai's company-specific work practices, those used in its plants in Korea as well as in its foreign plants, differ in significant ways from the 'Toyota model'. While Hyundai makes use of some aspects of the Toyota lean production methods, a number of Hyundai's work and production practices differ from Toyota's practices. Hyundai, for example, does not appear to rely on the tightly coupled supply chains found in Toyota, and Hyundai's shop floor practices include a more hierarchical, less team-oriented, more low-cost, and high-turnover focus than the practices found in Toyota.

Given the recent success of Hyundai in the global auto marketplace, it is fitting to try to identify the source of Hyundai's competitive strength as well as to take note of the fact that Hyundai appears to be succeeding without recourse to the strict Toyota method. I am struck by the fact that Hyundai's competitive strategy – a focus on low-cost and hierarchical work practices – bears some similarity to the competitive strategy long pursued by US auto makers which, interestingly, has not worked to the advantage of the US auto producers in recent years. The exact nature of Hyundai's competitive strengths in the global auto market and assessment of whether this advantage is sustainable in the long run, in the face of the strong recent performance of the Toyota Motor Corporation, are issues that deserve more attention.

Other key questions raised by the ongoing expansion of MNCs in the auto and other industries concern the structure and locus of the control of human resource and industrial relations decisions inside MNCs. Previous research on MNCs highlights the fact that traditionally human resource and industrial relations issues were among the most internally decentralised of corporate functions. In the face of historical, legal, cultural and political differences across countries that have critical effects on human resource and industrial relations practices and performance, MNCs traditionally left decision-making authority on HR and IR to local managers, often at the plant level. This in turn contributed to the wide variance apparent within MNCs in their human resource and industrial relations practices across their expanding production operations. Yet, many researchers, including myself, have claimed that in recent years there is a movement towards more centralisation within some MNCs in the control of HR and IR decision making. Furthermore, there has been the emergence of more regional and global structures, within those MNCs, in the face of more global markets, global supply chains and efforts to integrate production systems within the corporation.

This volume suggests that Hyundai never pursued the more local control of HR and IR decisions traditionally characteristic of other MNCs. It appears that due to Hyundai's corporate culture of hierarchical and tight control, corporate managers at Hyundai always maintained central control of HR and IR matters and continue to do so. Nor does the account of Hyundai's India plant suggest that this corporate-level control is shifting much in recent years. One could ponder whether the stability in the locus of control of HR and IR issues within Hyundai is due to something special about Hyundai's strategy and structure, or whether it is due to the fact that Hyundai's product or production strategies make it less sensitive to the kinds of pressures that are leading some other MNCs to shift to a more regional and/or global internal structure of HR and IR. On this and many other important questions, this volume by Russell Lansbury and his colleagues provides an excellent basis for discussion and a prompt for future work. Their contribution is much appreciated.

Harry C. Katz
Dean and the Jack Sheinkman Professor
School of Industrial and Labor Relations
Cornell University, Ithaca, New York

Notes

3 The Korean auto industry goes global

1 The emergence of a massive independent trade union movement since 1987 resulted in sharp rise of labour costs. Average wages in the manufacturing sector increased from US$296 per month in 1984 to US$723 in 1989 (Kwon and Suh 1998). Furthermore, the Korean won appreciated from 827.4 won to 679.6 won to (to US$1) during the same period (The Bank of Korea 1997).

2 Dunning (1993) explains these three motives as market-seeking, trade-seeking and strategic-asset-seeking FDI. See also Suh *et al.* (2000).

3 This can be explained by the theory put forward by Knickerbocker, who explained FDI in terms of rivalry and oligopolistic behaviours (1973).

4 Among them, the four largest conglomerates, Hyundai, LG, Samsung and Daewoo, accounted for more than half of South Korea's debt (Hankyoreh Newspaper 24 Mar. 1998).

5 For example, exchange rate of foreign currency against US$1 rose from 844.2 won in 1996 to 1415.2 won in December 1997 (Kwon and O'Donnell 1999: 278).

6 This is partly due to the rapid appreciation of the Japanese Yen after the Plaza accord.

7 During this period, the automobile exports from Japan also declined from 2,363,000 units in 1992 to 1,301,000 units in 1995. However, the cars produced in the United States increased substantially (Song 1998: 176–178).

8 Adopted from Moon (1995). Moon states the Korean path as 'Import Substitution – Exports to DCs – Exports to LDCs – Production in DCs – Production in LDCs'. However, HMC's investment in Canada was closed down only two years after its operation (Lansbury and Woo 2002).

9 Similar experiences can be found in the expansion of exports by the Korean electronics industry, which exported microwaves and colour TV sets even before they began to sell in the domestic markets (Steers *et al.* 1989).

10 John Dunning summarised these as 'the Paradoxes in Global capitalism' (Dunning 1998).

11 See Chapters 4 and 5 for the details of the production system in HMC and HMI.

12 Hyundai had several technical alliances with smaller companies in Japan, the United States and Europe.

13 However, these four periods mainly indicate the beginning of new major activities, which overlap with one another.

14 Although Daewoo began producing the cars in Eastern Europe in 1996, its operations faced serious difficulties due to the bankruptcy of the parent company in 1998. Closures of some subsidiaries of Daewoo after the 1997 economic crisis may not necessarily indicate their inefficient operation.

15 See Lansbury and Woo (2002), for the comparison of HMC Canada and HMI.

16 Daewoo also started production in Poland and Romania in 1996. However, they are experiencing difficulties after the 1997 economic crisis.
17 Chapter 6 explains this in detail.

4 Hyundai Motors as a global auto company

1 For example, total sales of Hyundai Business Group, organised by over 60 subsidiaries and 200,000 employees, was over 18 per cent of Korea's GDP (Gross Domestic Products: US$461.8 billion) in 1996 (*Weekly Chosun* 5 Jun. 1997, Hyundai Group Public Relations 1997, *Chosun Ilbo* 7 Dec. 1998).
2 HMC and its automobile subsidiaries planed to separate from Hyundai in late 2000, HECC and its subsidiaries and HHI and its subsidiaries in 2003 (*Chosun Ilbo* 20–31 Mar. 2000).
3 For example, if HMC is separated from the Hyundai Business Group, it is expected that HMC will no longer to enjoy its low cost of material supply from other Hyundai companies.
4 In 1988, 88 per cent of its total export sales were to the United States (HMC 1992: 751).
5 At this time, although body welding and metal lines were separated in the production chart, in practice, it was regarded as one line (HMC 1987: 70).
6 These machines and equipment were two powered fork lifts, one air compressor, 'one-set' of down draft spray booths and enamel oven, one portable spot welding equipment for *Cortina* folder, 'one-set' of fixed press welders, 'one-set' of *Cortina* assembly fixtures, 'one-set' of truck assembly fixtures and one portable spot welding gun for D-Service trucks (HMC 1987: 63–64).
7 In 1974, HMC employed various foreign technological advisors from the United Kingdom and the United States and allocated them in chassis engineering, body design and production, development and test, die and tooling, engine parts and so on (HMC 1992: 387–388).
8 Furthermore, the first model of HMC was developed according to Japanese standards, especially on the basis of the Mitsubishi *Lancer*, because of HMC's large dependence on the auto parts of Mitsubishi.
9 The job suggestion system was to promote technological developments and cost savings through the creativity of employees (HMC 1992: 462–463).
10 These were the *Excel* series (1,439cc), the *Sonata* series (1,800cc and 2,000cc), the *Grandeur* series (2,400cc and 3,000cc) and the *Elantra* and *Scope* series (1,600cc and 2,000cc).
11 Before this organisation, HECC's planning unit played its role to control business and management activities over various subsidiary companies of Hyundai.
12 For example, despite its balanced membership, the final decision required a two-third majority support of members. Furthermore, members were *appointed* by the management and confirmed by the government.
13 For further information in relation to this issue, see Kwon and O'Donnell (1999) and Choi (1989).
14 At the Hyundai Mipo Dockyard, official documents for the registration of its union were forcibly seized by management, despite the presence of government officials. In May 1988, a president of an HECC trade union branch in the managerial sector was kidnapped by management-backed terrorists and forced to resign from HECC. These events directly triggered a militant resistance from other workers and events such as these attracted nationwide attention and debate (*Donga Newspaper* 2 Jun. 1988, *Shin Donga* Jul. 1988: 375–393).

Bibliography

Automobile Manufactures Association of Korea (1983) *Hankuk Jadongcha Johab 20nyeonsa* (20 Years of Automobile Manufacturers Association of Korea), Seoul: AMAK.

Babson, S. (1992) *Lean or Mean: The MIT Model and Lean Production at Mazda*, Detroit, MI: Wayne State University Press.

Bae, Kyuhan (1983) *Automobile Workers in Korea*. Seoul: Seoul National University.

Bamber, G.J., Lansbury, R.D. and Wailes, N. (eds) (2004) *International and Comparative Employment Relations*, London: Sage.

Bank of Korea (1983) *Economic Statistics Year Book*. Seoul: Bank of Korea.

Bartlett, C. and Ghoshal, S. (1987) 'Managing across borders: new strategic requirements', *Sloan Management Review*, 28(4): 7–17.

Belis-Bergouignan, M., Bordenave, G. and Lung, Y. (1998) 'Global strategies in the automotive industry', *Actes du Gerpisa*, 18: 99–115.

Bhattacherjee, D. (2001) 'The evolution of Indian industrial relations: a comparative perspective', *Industrial Relations Journal*, 32(3): 244–263.

Boyer, R. and Freyssenet, M. (1995) 'The emergence of new industrial models', *Third GERPISA International Colloquium on New Industrial Models*, Paris, June.

Boyer, R. and Freyssenet, M. (2001) 'The world that changed the machine: synthesis of GERPISA research programs 1993–1999', *Actes du Gerpisa,* 31: 4–8.

Boyer, R., Freyssenet, M. and Lung, R. (1996) 'Between globalisation and regionalisation: what choices for the automobile industry?' *La Lettre du Gerpisa*, 102, Apr.

Bray, M. and Lansbury, R.D. (2000) 'The conditions for convergence: multinationals, product markets, production systems and employment relations', *Journal of Industrial Relations*, 42(2): 295–313.

Bray, M. and Murray, G. (2000) 'Globalization and labour regulation', *Journal of Industrial Relations*, 42(2): 167–172.

Calabrese, G. (2001) 'The globalisation of research and development in the car industry', *International Journal of Automotive Technology and Management*, 1(1): 145-159.

Cantwell, J. (1991) 'A Survey of theories of international production', in C. Pitelis and R. Sugden (eds) *The Nature of the Transnational Firm*, London: Routledge, 16–63.

Cho, Hyorae and Park, Jonggue (1989) 'Joseonsanyeob (Shipbuilding industry)', in Lee, Junghee (ed.) *Dogjeom Daekieobkwa Nodongwundong 2* (The Large Scale and Monopolistic Company and the Labour Movement II), Seoul: Baeksan.

Choi, Jangjip (1989) *Labor and the Authoritarian State: Labor Unions in South Korean Manufacturing Industries*. Seoul: Korea University Press.

Deyo, F. (ed.) (1996) *Social Reconstructions of the World Automobile Industry: Competition, Power and Industrial Flexibility*, London: St. Martins Press.

Doleschal, R. (1992) 'Internationalisation and the reorganisation of production and marketing in the Volkswagen corporation', in W.D. Graf (ed.) *The Internationalisation of the German Economy*, London: St. Martins Press.

Drury, G. (2001) 'Automotive locations buckle up for an uncertain future', *Corporate Location*, Mar./Apr.

Dunning, J.H. (1977) 'Trade, location of economic activity and the MNE: a search for an eclectic approach', in B.O. Hesselborn and P.M. Wijkman (eds) *The International Allocation of Economic Activity*, New York: Holmes and Meier Publishers.

Dunning, J.H. (1988) 'The eclectic paradigm of international production: a restatement and some possible extensions', *Journal of International Business Studies*, 19(1): 1–32.

Dunning, J.H. (1993) *Multinational Enterprises and Global Economy*, Beccles: Addison-Wesley Publishing Co.

Dunning, J.H. (1995) 'Reappraising the eclectic paradigm in an age of alliance capitalism', *Journal of International Business Studies*, 26(3): 461–491.

Dunning, J.H. (1998) 'Location and the multinational enterprise: a neglected factor?' *Journal of International Business Studies*, 29: 45–66.

Ealey, L. and Troyano-Bermudez, L. (2000) 'The automotive industry: a 30,000-mile checkup', *McKinsey Quarterly*, 1: 72–79.

Edwards, T., Rees, C. and Coller, X. (1999) 'Structure, politics and the diffusion of employment relations in multinationals', *European Journal of Industrial Relations*, 5(3): 286–306.

Ferner, A. and Edwards, P. (1995) 'Power and the diffusion of organisational change within multinational enterprises', *European Journal of Industrial Relations*, 1(2): 229–258.

Frenkel, S.J. (1994) 'Patterns of workplace relations in the global corporation: towards convergence?' in J. Belanger, P. Edwards and L. Haiven (eds) *Workplace Industrial Relations and the Global Challenge*, Ithaca, NY: Cornell University Press, 240–274.

Freyssenet, M. (1996) 'The recomposition of the economic and political world environment', *La Lettre du Gerpisa*, 106(Oct.): 2–6.

Freyssenet, M. and Lung, Y. (2000) 'Between globalisation and regionalisation: what is the future of the automobile industry?' in J. Humphrey, Y. Lecler and M. Salerno (eds) *Global Strategies and Local Realities: The Auto Industry in Emerging Markets*, London: Macmillan.

Garibaldo, F. and Battaglini, E. (1998) 'Mobility and environment: is it possible to transfer Western mobility patterns to emerging countries?' *Actes du Gerpisa*, 28: 93–103.

Hatzfeld, N. (1998) 'The Asian crisis and Japanese automobile constructors', *La Lettre du Gerpisa*, 127(Dec.): 5–6.

HECC (Hyundai Engineering and Construction Corporation) (1982) *Hyundai Geonseol 35yeonsa* (A Thirty-five Year History of Hyundai Engineering and Construction), Seoul: HECC.

Herzenberg, S. (1996) 'Regulatory frameworks and developments in the North American auto industry', in F. Deyo (ed.) *Social Reconstructions of the World Automobile Industry: Competition, Power and Industrial Flexibility*, London: St. Martins Press, 261–294.

HHI (Hyundai Heavy Industries) (1992) *Hyundai Junggongeobsa* (History of Hyundai Heavy Industries), Seoul: HHI.

Hill, R.C. and Lee, Y.C. (1998) 'Japanese multinationals and East Asian development: the case of the automobile industry', in L. Sklair (ed.) *Capitalism and Development*, London: Routledge.

HMC (Hyundai Motor Company) (1987) *Hyundai Jadongcha 20yeonsa* (A Twenty Year History of Hyundai Motor Company), Seoul: HMC

HMC (Hyundai Motor Company) (1992) *Hyundai Jadongchasa* (The History of the Hyundai Motor Company), Seoul: HMC.

Howell, L. and Hsu, J. (2002) 'Globalisation within the auto industry', *Research Technology Management*, Jul.–Aug.: 43–49.

Humphrey, J. (2000) 'Assembler–supplier relations in the auto industry: globalisation and national development', *Competition and Change*, 4: 245–271.

Hyun, I.-G. (1991) 'Internationalization of the Korean automobile industry: some strategic planning', *PhD Thesis*, Department of International Trade and Business, Graduate School, Hankuk University of Foreign Studies.

International Metalworkers Federation (IMF) (1995) *Unions and the Auto Industry in the Asian-Pacific Region*, Geneva: IMF.

International Metalworkers Federation (IMF) (2000) *IMF Auto Report 2000*, Geneva: IMF.

Johanson, J. and Vanhne, J.-E. (1977) 'The internationalization process of the firm: a model of knowledge development and increasing foreign market commitments', *Journal of International Business Studies*, 8(1): 23–32.

Kang, Sudol (1987) 'Saengsankisuleui Nodongtongjaemit Nodongeuisikae Kwanhan Yeongu (A study of the production system, labour conrol and labourers' conciousness)', *Master Thesis*, Department of Economics, Seoul: Seoul National University.

Katz, H. and Darbishire, O. (2000) *Converging Divergences: Worldwide Change in Employment Systems*, Ithaca, NY: Cornell University Press.

Kenney, M. and Florida, R. (1993) *Beyond Mass Production: The Japanese System and its Transfer to the US*, New York: Oxford University Press.

Kim, H.-K. (1995) 'The global strategy of the Korean automobile industry', *Masters Thesis*, Graduate School of Business Administration, Seoul: Yonsei University.

Kim, Hyeoungki (1988) *Hankukui Dokjeomjabonkwa Imnodong* (Monopolistic Capitalism in Korea and Wage Labour), Seoul: Kkachi.

Kim, Wangun (1993) '1980 yeondae Hankukjadongchasaneobeui Baljeonyangsik Byeonea Kwanhan Yaeongu (Changes in the development stages of the Korean automobile industry)', *PhD Thesis*, Department of Sociology, Pusan: Pusan National University.

Kim, Y.-S. (1996) 'A study on the globalization process of Korean automobile industry', *Masters Thesis*, Graduate School of Business Administration, Seoul: Yonsei University.

Knickerbocker, F.T. (1973) *Oligopolistic Reaction and Multinational Enterprise*, Boston, MA: Harvard Business School Press.

Kochan, T.A., Lansbury, R.D. and MacDuffie, J.P. (eds) (1997) *After Lean Production: Evolving Employment Practices in the World Auto Industry*, New York: Cornell University Press.

Kogut, B. and Zander, U. (1993) 'Knowledge of the firm and the evolutionary theory of the multinational corporation', *Journal of International Business Studies*, 24(4): 625–645.

Kong, Jaewuk (1992) *Hankuk Jabonjueiwa Chaebol* (Korean Capitalism and the Chaebol), Seoul: Munhakkwa Jiseong.

Korea Automobile Manufacturers Association (1987) *Annual Report*, Seoul: AMAK.

Korea Automobile Manufacturers Association (various issues) *Korean Automobile Industry*, Various issues from 1993–2002, Seoul.

Korean Industrial Bank (1984) *Industrial Statistics Year Book*. Seoul: KIB.

Kwon, S. and O'Donnell, M. (1999) 'Repression and struggle: the state, the chaebol and independent trade unions in South Korea', *Journal of Industrial Relations*, 41(2): 272–293.

Kwon, S. and O'Donnell, M. (2001) *The Chaebol and Labour in Korea: The Development of Management Strategy in Hyundai*, London: Routledge.

Kwon, S. and Suh, C.-S. (1998) 'Growth strategy and structure of the Korean Chaebol: the Hyundai business group, from the 1940s to the IMF crisis', *4th Pacific and Asia conference on Korean Studies, Korea between Tradition and Modernity*, University of British Columbia, Vancouver, Canada, 10–13 May.

Kwon, S. and Suh, C.-S. (2003) 'The Chaebol and Korean capitalism: the Hyundai business group', in M.J. Tcha and C.-S. Suh (eds) *The Economic Crisis and the Korean Economy at the Crossroads*, London: Routledge, 127–152.

Kwon, S., Rhee, D.-K. and Suh, C.-S. (2004) 'Globalization strategies of South Korean electronics companies after the 1997 financial crisis', *Asia Pacific Business Review*, Special Issue, 10(3/4): 422–440.

Laigle, L. (1995) 'De la sous-traitance classique au co-developpement', *Actes du GERPISA*, 14: 23–40.

Lansbury, R.D. and Woo, S. (2002) 'Technological innovation, production strategies and human resources in the Korean auto industry', *International Conference on Science, Technology and Innovation: Emerging International Policy Issues*, Centre for International Development, Harvard University, USA, 23–24 Sep.

Lansbury, R.D., Lee, B.-H. and Woo, S.-H. (2004) 'Technology, human resources and international competitiveness in the Korean auto industry: the case of Kia Motors', *International Journal of Technology and Globalisation*, 1(1): 119–129.

Lansbury, R.D., Kwon, S.-H. and Suh, C.-S. (2006) 'Globalization and employment relation in the known auto Industry: The case of the Hyundai Motor Company in Korea, Canada and India', *Asia Pacific Business Review*, 12(2): 131–147

Lee, Jongseon (1989) 'Jungkongeob Geodaedogjeomkieobeaseoeui Nodongwundongea Kwanhan Yeongu (The labour movements in large scale and monopolistic heavy industries)', *Master Thesis*, Department of Sociology, Seoul: Korea University.

Lee, Younghee (1994) *Fordism and Post-Fordism.*, Seoul: Hanol.

Lung, Y. (1998) 'Is the rise of emerging countries as automotive producers an irreversible phenomenon?' *Actes du Gerpisa*, 28: 7–19.

Lung, Y. (2001) 'The co-ordination of competencies and knowledge: a critical issue for regional automotive systems', *Actes du Gerpisa*, 31: 7–18.

MacDuffie, J.P. (1995) 'International trends in work organisation in the international auto industry: national-level versus company-level perspectives', in K. Wever and L. Turner (eds) *The Comparative Political Economy of Industrial Relations*, Madison, WI: IRRA, 71–114.

MacDuffie, J.P. and Pil, F. (1997) 'Changes in auto industry employment practices: an international overview', in T.A. Kochan, R.D. Lansbury and J.P. MacDuffie (eds) *After Lean Production: Evolving Employment Practices in the World Auto Industry*, New York: Cornell University Press, 9–44.

Mair, A. (1994) *Honda's Global Local Corporation*, Basingstoke: Macmillan.

Maxcy, G. (1981) *The Multinational Motor Industry*, London: Croom Helm.

Miller, R. (1994) 'Global research and development networks and large-scale innovations: the case of the automobile industry', *Research Policy*, 23: 27–46.

Moon, H.-C. (1997) 'A new theory of explaining FDI motivations of Korean firms', *Academy of International Business Annual Meeting*, Monterrey, Mexico.

Moon, H.-C. and Roehl, T.W. (1993) 'An imbalance theory of foreign direct investment', *Multinational Business Review*, Spring: 56–65.

Moon, H.-C. and Roehl, T.W. (2001) 'Unconventional foreign direct investment and imbalance theory', *International Business Review*, 10(3).

Moon, Won Suk. (1995) 'An analysis of the process of globalisation of the Korean automobile industry and its problems', Sangkyungnonjib, Seoul (in Korean), pp. 90–120.

Oh, Woncheol (1996) *Hankukhyeong Kyungjae Keunseol* (Korean Type of Economic Development), Seoul: Kia Research Institute.

Ohmae, K. (1990) *The Borderless World*, London: Collins.

Owen, G. (2000) 'What's Ford driving at?' *Management Today*, Oct.

Park, Funku (1982) 'Choseon Kongyeob (Shipbuilding industries)', in Kim, Soogon and Ha, Taehgon (eds) *Nosakwangae Saraejib* (Case Studies on Industrial Relations), Seoul: Korean Development Institute.

Park, Joonshik (1991) 'Junggongeob Daegieobeseoui Nosakwangyeye Gwanhanyeongu (The industrial relations patterns in heavy industry companies: the case of steel and shipbuilding corporations)', *PhD Thesis*, Department of Sociology, Seoul: Yonsei University.

Piore, M. and Sabel, C. (1984) *The Second Industrial Divide*, New York: Basic Books.

Porter, M. (1990) *The Competitive Advantage of Nations*, New York: The Free Press.

PricewaterhouseCoopers (2000a) *Automotive Sector Insights: Analysis and Opinions on Merger and Acquisition Activity*, [online] available at: http://www.pwcglobal.com/insights/auto

PricewaterhouseCoopers (2000b) *The Second Automotive Century*, [online] available at: http://www.pwcglobal.com

Roh, Honghyeong (1992) 'Jadongchasaneui Jadonghwawa Nodongkwajeongeui Byeonhwaea Kwanhan Yeongu (Automation and changes in the labour process in the automobile industry)', *Master Thesis*, Department of Sociology, Seoul: Seoul National University.

Rugman, A.M. and D'Cruz, J.R. (1993) 'The "Double Diamond" model of international - competitiveness: the Canadian experience', *Management International Review*, 33(2): 29–35.

Saddler, D. (1999) 'Internationalisation and specialisation in the European automotive components sector: implications for the hollowing-out thesis', *Regional Studies*, 33(2).

Santucci, M. (1997) 'Globalisation of the auto parts industry', *Journal of International Marketing*, 5(3): 85–89.

Seo, J.-S. and Suh, C.-S. (1999) 'Location advantages of foreign direct investment in East Asia', *Academy of International Business Annual Meeting, The Janus Face of Globalization*, Charleston, SC, 20–23 Nov.

Song, Il (1998) 'The process of globalisation of the Korean automobile industry: with a focus on a comparison between Korea and Japan', *Economics and Management Analysis*, 18(1) (in Korean).

Spatz, J. and Nunnenkamp, P. (2002) 'Globalisation of the automobile industry: traditional locations under pressure?' *Kiel Working Paper No. 1093.*

Steers, R.M., Shin, Y.K. and Ungson, G.R. (1989) *The Chaebol: Korea's New Industrial Might*, New York: Harper Collins Publishers.

Subramaniam, M. and Venkatraman, N. (2001) 'Determinants of transnational new product development capbility: testing the influence of transferring and deploying tacit overas knowledge', *Strategic Management Journal*, 22: 359–378.

Suh, C.-S. and Seo, J.-S. (1998) 'Trends in foreign direct investment: the case of the Asia-Pacific region', in A. Levy (ed.) *Handbook on the Globalisation of the World Economy*, Cheltenham: Edward Elgar, 123–146.

Suh, C.-S. and Seo, J.-S. (1999) 'Foreign direct investment in East Asia: a comparison between European, American and Asian investments', in S.-G. Lee and P.-B. Ruffini (eds) *The Global Integration of Europe and East Asia: Studies of International Trade and Investment*, Cheltenham: Edward Elgar, 171–186.

Suh, C.-S., Seo, J.-S. and Moon, H.-C. (2000) 'The dynamic relationship between ownership and location advantages of foreign direct investment', *KAREC Discussion Paper* 2(4), Korea–Australasia Research Centre, University of New South Wales.

Teece, D. (1998) 'Capturing value from knowledge assets: the new economy, markets for know-how, and intangible assets', *California Management Review*, 40(3): 55–79.

Teece, D., Pisano, G. and Shuen, A. (1997) 'Dynamic capabilities and strategic management', *Strategic Management Journal*, 18(7): 509–533.

The Bank of Korea (1997) *Kiubkyeongyeongbunseok* 1997 (Financial Statement Analysis for 1997) Seoul.

The Korea Federation of Banks (2002) *Overseas Direct Investment Statistics Yearbook*, Seoul.

UNCTAD (1998) *World Investment Report 1998: Trends and Determinations*, New York: United Nations.

UNCTAD (1999) *World Investment Report 1999: Foreign Direct Investment and the Challenge of Development*, New York: United Nations.

Venkata Ratnam, C.S. (1995) 'Economic liberalisation and the transformation of industrial relations policies in India', in A. Verma, T.A. Kochan and R.D. Lansbury (eds) *Employment Relations in the Growing Asian Economies*, London: Routledge, 248–314.

Vickery, G. (1996) 'Globalisation in the automobile industry', in OECD (ed.) *The Globalisation of Industry*, Paris: Organisation for Economic Cooperation and Development, 153–205.

Wade, R. (1996) 'Globalisation and its limits: reports of the death of the national economies are greatly exaggerated', in S. Berger and R. Dore (eds) *National Diversity and Global Capitalism*, Ithaca, NY: Cornell University Press.

Williams, K., Haslam, C., Johal, S. and Williams, J. (1994) *Cars: Analysis, History, Cases*, Providence: Berghahn Books.

Winter, S. (2000) 'The satisfying principle in capability learning', *Strategic Management Journal*, 21: 981–996.

Womack, J.P., Jones, D.T. and Ross, D. (1990) *The Machine that Changed the World*, New York: Rawson Associates.

World Trade Agenda (2000) *Global or Not: The Auto Sector Looks to Open to New Trade Disputes and Heavy Pressure on Market Opening and Investment Terms*, Geneva: World Trade Organisation.

Magazine

Monthly Mal Nov. 1987

Interviews – HGTUA

HGTUA officer, 9 Jul. 1994

Interviews – FMWU

FMWU senior officers, 27–28 Mar. 1999

Interviews – HECC

HECC foremen, 3 Jul. 1994

Interviews – HMI

HMI engineers, 8 Jul. 1999.
HMI engineer, 6 Sep. 2000.
HMI engineer, 9 Sep. 2000.
HMI foremen, 7 Jul. 1999.
HMI foremen, 10 Sep. 2000.
HMI personnel specialist, 10 Sep. 2000.
HMI production manager, 6 Jul. 1999.
HMI production manager, 6 Sep. 2000.
HMI skilled worker, 7 Jul. 1999.
HMI skilled worker, 8 Jul. 1999.
HMI TQC specialist, 8 Jul. 1999.
HMI TQC specialist, 7 Sep. 2000.
Senior manager in HMI Planning Office, 6 Jul. 1999.
Senior manager in HMI Planning Office, 6 Sep. 2000.
Senior manager in HMI Planning Office, 10 Sep. 2000.

Interviews – HMC

A former HMC Trade Union officer, 2 Apr. 1999
HMC engineers, 19 Apr. 1999.
HMC engineer, 2 Sep. 2000.
HMC foremen, 27 Mar. 2001.
HMC personnel specialist, 14 May 1998.
HMC personnel specialist, 10 Mar. 1999
HMC personnel specialist, 22 Feb. 2000.
HMC personnel specialist, 19 Apr. 1999.
HMC production manager, 14 May 1998.
HMC production manager, 9 Jan. 1999.
HMC production manager, 17 Apr. 1999.
HMC skilled worker, 20 Jul. 1994
HMC skilled worker, 14 May 1998.
HMC skilled worker, 2 Sep. 2000.
HMC TQC specialist, 24 Aug. 1994
HMC TQC specialist, 22 Feb. 2000.
HMC TQC specialist, 2 Sep. 2000.
HMC unionist, 4 Aug. 1994
HMC trade unionist, 2 Sep. 2000.
HMC trade unionists, 20 Dec. 2000.
HMC trade unionist, 27 Mar. 2001.
HMC Trade Union officer, 30 Mar. 1999
Senior manager in HMC Planning Office, 8 Jan. 1999.
Senior manager in HMC Planning Office, 19 Feb. 2000.

Company documents

HGTUA (1993) (Hyundai Group Trade Union Association) Hyundai Group Nomukwanri Siltae Bogoseo (A Report on the Labour Management Policies and Practices of the Hyundai Group), HGTUA internal sources.

HGTUA (1994) (Hyundai Group Trade Union Association) Hyunchongryeon Danhyeobjaryojib (Data for Collective Bargaining by the Hyundai Trade Union Association), HGTUA sources.

HMC (1998–2001a), Hyundai Jadongcha Insakwangae (Collection of documents of HMC human resource management practices), HMC internal sources.

HMC (1998–2001b), Hyundai Jadongcha Kyungyoungkwan (Collection of documents of HMC business strategies and practices), HMC internal sources.

HMC (1998–2001c), Hyundai Jadongcha Saengsankwanri Hwaldong (Collection of documents of HMC production management practices), HMC internal sources.

HMI (1999–2000a), Hyundai Jadongcha India Gongjang Insakwangae (Collection of documents of HMI human resource management practices), HMI internal sources.

HMI (1999–2000b), Hyundai Jadongcha India Gongjang Kyungyoungkwan (Collection of documents of HMI business strategies and practices), HMI internal sources.

HMI (1999–2000c), Hyundai Jadongcha India Gongjang Saengsankwanri Hwaldong (Collection of documents of HMI production management practices), HMI internal sources.

Hyundai Research Institute (Feb. 1990) Groupanae Gongaechaeyoungjaedo Munjaejeomkwa Daeyeung Bangan (Proposals for Improvements to the Open Recruitment System for Newcomers (University Graduates) of Hyundai Group), HRI: Seoul.

Index

DURHAM UNIVERSITY LIBRARY
3 0104 01570100 0